North

.

North

Lindsay Barrett

PUNCHER & WATTMANN

First published in 2023
Published by Puncher and Wattmann
PO Box 279
Waratah NSW 2298

https://www.puncherandwattmann.com
web@puncherandwattmann.com

ISBN   9781922571717

Cover image, 'Kogarah boys' by Des Matejka 1973.
Cover design by Miranda Douglas
Typesetting by Morgan Arnett
Printed by Lightning Source International

NATIONAL LIBRARY OF AUSTRALIA

A catalogue record for this work is available from the National Library of Australia

For Mark

In memory of Kevin Peacock (1959-2015)

'Intelligence is the ability to harness the powers of the surrounding world without destroying the said world.'

Arkady and Boris Strugatsky
Roadside Picnic

'The east coast of Australia used to be one big, contiguous forest.'

Raina Plowright, Ecologist and Epidemiologist, in David Quammen,
Spillover: Animal Infections and the Next Human Pandemic, 2012

1

For a long time my friend Lachlan had been trying to get me to make a trip up north.

So, on an overcast January morning I was loading the back of my Ford station wagon with the items necessary for a long journey on the road: a sleeping bag and a plastic groundsheet; a small overnight bag with a couple of extra pairs of shorts, singlets and t-shirts; a battered and blackened billy and some enamelled mugs from which to drink the tea brewed in the billy; a jaffle iron; some plastic plates and a few knives and forks; a canvas bag full of fishing lines; an axe that had belonged to my grandfather who'd grown up in the bush near Braidwood; a spare pair of thongs, and an ex-Army jerry can full of water: useful for drinking, filling the billy and for refilling the car's radiator when it boiled over.

I went and said goodbye to my Aunt Millie (my father's aunt actually), who lived next door. She was over eighty and was the only person I knew who had been born in the nineteenth century. She wished me well and a safe trip. I felt a little sad leaving her, as I took her to the small supermarket in Arncliffe to do her shopping once a week, but all the same, my father would be able to stand-in, as he had been the one to take her before I'd learned to drive. Still, it played on my mind: taking Millie shopping was my only real responsibility or commitment in life.

I got into the Ford, turned the key in the ignition, listened to the engine kick over, and backed out into the street. I was twenty-one years old.

I drove over to pick up Gordie, Gordon Fraser, from the blond brick villa in which he lived with his parents and older brother. He was waiting out the front with his own small bag of travelling gear, dressed in thongs, a pair of black shorts and a bright red Sex Pistols t-shirt from which he'd ripped off the sleeves. God Save the Queen was spelt out across his chest in the mock-ransom-note font so loved by punk designers.

Gordie got into the car and we turned around and backtracked to pick up Kevin, who only lived a few streets away from me but whose home was technically further north than mine and therefore was our last stop before properly heading off. Kevin too was waiting in his thongs and shorts and t-shirt, though his was a shirt that made no statement, it was just a plain pale blue. Kevin was quite fat and had lately grown a pencil moustache as some sort of affectation of distinction. Actually he'd been rather unstable for the past year or so, a state of affairs we put down to a combination of the distress of his parents' divorce a couple of years earlier and the taking of too much of the acid for which he'd acquired a taste while working alongside a part-time drug dealer in the Department of Veterans' Affairs in the city.

Not that he was working in the public service now; he'd resigned a few months ago. Actually, none of us had proper jobs. Gordie did casual work at the railway workshops at Eveleigh, which essentially meant clocking on a couple of days a week and then finding a carriage to snooze in for most of the day until it was time to clock off. I, meanwhile, had just finished the second year of a teaching degree, though the word finished gives a much greater sense of accomplishment on my part than was actually the case. As it was, I wasn't sure if I was going to drop out or if they were going to kick me out. Only time would tell.

And as for Lachlan, the spiritual father of this journey, well he was already in Queensland, waiting supposedly, with our other mates Albert and Alka, at Scarborough in Brisbane at the home of a bloke called Glen and his missus Louise.

I pulled up outside Kevin's house and he sauntered over, opened the tailgate, threw his bag in with the rest of the stuff and then climbed into the back seat. Then I started up the Ford again, drove to the end of Kevin's street and turned right onto the Princes Highway and headed north.

2

This was not our first attempt to travel to North Queensland. Two years earlier we'd planned another trip to Cairns, Albert and I in my car and Lachlan and another friend called Benny in his old Volvo. Benny was very taken with what to me seemed the quite crazy idea that it was better to leave at midnight and drive through the night, because there was less traffic, than it was to travel during the day. I wanted no part of this. In fact, Kevin and I had tried it ourselves once, with the aim of visiting his cousin, who was at Uni in Armidale. We'd watched television for a couple of hours (*A Night to Remember*, with Kenneth Moore as the First Officer of the *Titanic*) and had then gotten into the car and headed off. But by the time we reached Maitland we were so dead tired we turned around and drove home.

Nonetheless, Lachlan was drawn to the idea of a midnight departure – he was always one for grand or dramatic gestures – so he and Benny had duly left in the middle of the evening dark, with the intention that Al and I would depart the next morning and that we would meet at some point further on up the coast.

It must have been about 2am when my father gently shook me by the shoulder, waking me from a deep sleep. Lachlan had just telephoned. He and Benny had been in an accident. Benny was in hospital with a broken leg. Lachlan wasn't hurt, but he was going to have to spend the night in a cell at the police station at Belmont because there was nowhere else for him to stay.

I went back to bed and back to sleep but woke up early the next morning and phoned Al to tell him I'd be over to pick him up soon. By midday we'd collected Lachlan from the police station and were standing around Benny's hospital bed in Newcastle. His right leg had been shattered, and a surgeon had opened up the side of it and inserted a cantilevered metal pin that ran from his hip to his shin. It would be some time before he'd walk again, and he'd probably have a permanent limp. Lucky he'd been driving a Volvo, everyone agreed.

A Land Cruiser full of drunken local fishermen had made a turn across their path. Benny had swerved, but not enough to avoid the collision. None of the fishermen had been hurt. Because he was a local, the police had given the driver an infringement notice but had then let him leave the scene of the accident without a breath test. This was no consolation to Benny (a probationary police constable himself, a fact of which the attending cops were unaware), who certainly wouldn't be seeing Queensland any time soon.

Later that afternoon we left Benny and his woes in the hospital and drove back down the coast. Past the last of the southern Newcastle suburbs we turned off the highway, following a dirt road through the coastal national park to a place called Bongon Beach. We couldn't stop chuckling over the designation, it was if it had been named just for us, and as soon as we stopped the car at the campground Lachlan pulled out a foil and made up a mix of heads and tobacco while Al got out the bong he'd made from an orange juice bottle and a piece of garden hose, something he was more or less an expert at. Then we pulled a few cones and talked over the situation. Benny, we agreed through a haze of smoke, was well and truly fucked. But obviously, he'd want us to continue with our trip. Wouldn't he? Of course he would. So we resolved to stay for a few days, visit him a few more times and then go on our way.

It was starting to get dark by the time we'd sorted out our priorities, so we stumbled around collecting bits of wood and then Al got a fire going while Lachlan and I put up the tent. A combination of the darkness and the fact that we were seriously stoned meant that we kept sticking the wrong pieces of tent pole together and forgetting to hammer in the pegs, but eventually, we got the job done. Then we sat around the flickering fire for a little while, but it had been a long day and Lachlan and I soon crawled under the canvas and into our sleeping bags. Al stayed by the fire, staring into the flames reflecting on something or other. There was nothing unusual in this. He did it a lot.

The next morning the blue sky was full of puffy white clouds. The beach was really quite beautiful in the daylight. The surf was miserly, but this didn't really matter because we didn't have surfboards, we'd been intending to go to far North Queensland after all. We went up to the café at the petrol station on the highway near the beach road turnoff, the Big T it was called in an obvious effort to appeal to truck drivers, and had a breakfast of bacon and eggs and then went to visit Benny again. Then we went back down to the sea and had a swim in amongst the small waves. It wasn't too difficult a rhythm to settle into.

3

A couple of days later on the beach we met a young woman, Denise. She was a nurse at a North Shore hospital and had four days off after a week of night shifts. She'd set up her tent on a rise overlooking the ocean at the other end of the beach. It was only October but her freckly skin was dry and brown and her dishevelled chestnut hair was sun-bleached in streaks. If she'd learned about melanoma in the course of her training, it hadn't seemed to bother her.

The next afternoon we were sitting around our campsite smoking a joint after having come back from yet another visit to Benny when Denise appeared. A man had come out of the bush and sat himself down outside her tent. There was something strange about him, she said, and he wouldn't go away. Would we come back with her and check him out? Maybe our presence would give him the hint to leave.

We finished the joint and stumbled up the hill with her and sure enough, planted cross-legged on the ground next to Denise's small tent was the bloke in question. He was blond and plump and reminded me of the entrepreneur Alan Bond, famous at the time for buying up breweries and trying to win the America's Cup. However, the resemblance ended there, because he was wearing a lightweight short-sleeved cotton dressing gown, the sort that was worn in summer over shorty pyjamas, but that was all he was wearing, and it wasn't done up in front. His mouth meanwhile was outlined in bright red lipstick and glassy chandelier-like earrings hung from both ears. It would have been interesting to have seen what colour his eyes were, but they were hidden behind a pair of sunglasses with enormous smoky-brown lenses.

We said hello and sat down opposite, I for one trying to avoid staring at his languid genitals. Des, he said his name was. I was a little confused, despite the lipstick and the earrings he didn't appear to be in drag as such, and so I couldn't really work out where he was coming from. What are ya' up to, mate, Lachlan asked? Just havin' a bit of a bushwalk, Des said by way of an explanation. He seemed happy enough to talk, he was probably used to such abrupt and direct questions, I reasoned, if he got around looking like this.

We chatted away about the weather and the local landscape and the nearby beaches. Des appeared to consider it the most commonplace thing in the world to be gadding about the bush in dressing gown, lippie and earrings. And, while it may have seemed utterly bizarre to the rest of us, really, who were we to argue. Anyway, the point of the meeting was to discourage him from getting too comfortable around Denise, and this we seemed to have achieved, because after a while he excused himself and got up and wandered back into the bush. Fucking hell, what a *unit*, we all agreed, as the bright oranges and yellows of his gown blended into the undergrowth.

We invited Denise back down to our camp for a cup of tea. She ended up sitting with us and smoking joints long into the night and when she finally announced that it was time for her to go back up to her tent Lachlan quickly volunteered himself to walk her home, 'just in case.' I expected him to try it on her, it would have been out of character for him not to, but if he did, then he obviously received no warmer reception than had Des, because he was back within ten minutes, minus his customary self-satisfied smirk and with nothing much to say for himself.

We'd agreed to leave the next day. After our morning cup of tea I went down to the beach to have a last look around while Lachlan and Al fiddled at the campsite, pulling bongs and slowly packing up. I was happy to pass on this because, while I liked smoking dope, I didn't like it anywhere near as much as they did.

I was walking along the grassy rise at the back of the beach when a voice called to me. It was Denise, sheltering from the cool morning breeze in a sandy hollow underneath the grass verge. She was sitting on a blanket, facing the ocean and drinking red wine from a cardboard cask. I climbed down and sat on the rug next to her and she handed me a plastic cup, then filled it with wine from the cask. I took a sip. I never did this, drank wine on the beach in the morning, but it was great, and I wondered why I hadn't done it before now. It was a cloudless day, and sheltered from the wind it was almost warm, so I took off the flannelette shirt I had on over my t-shirt. Denise was already exposing her brown legs to the morning sun, and now she reached up and pulled off her cotton pullover, which left her naked except for a pair of bikini bottoms with a blue floral pattern. There was nothing revelatory in this, she'd spent all her time with us at the beach topless, but it was nice now to be in such close and intimate proximity to her nakedness. I looked for a moment at her velvety, dark pink nipples and at her smallish tan breasts before turning back to the ocean. I studied the line of the surf, but actually I could have looked at her breasts for hours.

I emptied my cup and she refilled it. We talked about our lives and what we wanted from them. She wanted to keep on with her nurse's training and specialise in trauma and intensive care. I on the other hand didn't know what I wanted. Actually, I was working off and on as a barman in clubs and pubs, and while I didn't intend to make a career out of such a dead end job, desires like Denise's didn't appeal to me at all. While I could perhaps see the allure of the adrenaline rush, I was absolutely certain that I myself didn't want anything to do with banged up people at death's door in hospital. Still, I was glad someone did, especially someone as beautiful and charming as Denise.

I lay back on the rug and stared through my sunglasses into the depthless sky. My gaze drifted to the side and I looked at Denise's brown freckle-covered back and listened to her chuckle at one of her own jokes. I had a vague memory of a scene just like this from a Carly Simon or James Taylor song, I couldn't remember which, but it was definitely something Californian. I closed my eyes and felt the warmth of the sun on my face and I felt absolutely content.

So that's where you are. We've been looking for you everywhere. I opened my eyes to see Al looking down from the grass verge. He said hello to Denise, then asked me if I was ready to go, because he and Lachlan had packed up the car. Was I ready to go? Ready to go? Of course not, all I wanted to do was lie in the sun with this almost-naked girl and drink wine. But I didn't have a choice, did I? For a start, it was my car and they needed me to drive it. Nor did I want to suggest we stay a bit longer because I had no intention of sharing this unexpected nirvana with the other two. So I told Al I'd be along in a few minutes. We said goodbye and Denise instructed me as to how to contact her when I got back to Sydney, but I knew I wouldn't be doing that, because I never was very good at that sort of thing.

4

By late afternoon we were in Port Macquarie. We parked the car and went to the supermarket and then looked around the shops. Al found a copy of Carlos Castaneda's *A Separate Reality* in the secondhand bookshop. I bought a dark green mohair jumper from the St. Vincent de Paul.

At dusk we crossed the river on the punt. It was a cool, perfectly still evening and the water looked as dark and viscous as oil as the punt slowly dragged itself and us and the rest of its cargo across to the opposite shore. A reddish orange glow on the horizon backlit the black shapes of the gum trees along the riverbanks further upstream.

We drove off the punt and into the dark and along the unsealed, potholed coast road until we came to a place called Big Hill and set up our tent in the light of the car's headlights. Then, as always, we got a fire going, and sat around it until it was time to go to sleep.

The next evening we went into the nearest big town, Kempsey, and went to the RSL for a steak and a beer. At the pool tables we met a balding man in his thirties called Robert. He had a bushy but perfectly trimmed moustache and a deep and mellifluous voice. Listen to this bloke, Lachlan said to me in an aside, he sounds like he's on the radio. Which in fact he was, he was in the middle of a six-month stint at the regional ABC station in Kempsey. He didn't have many friends in town, and he had the next day off, so we offered to return in the morning and pick him up from the pub where he was staying and take him down to the beach.

Which we did: it was a clear and beautiful spring day and we spent it mucking around in the surf and fishing off the rocks and going for a walk around the headland (the 'big' hill) and looking down at the bat-filled cave on the other side of which you could dive down and swim into at high tide if you were game. Then we lit a fire and sat around it and pulled bongs and drank beer. Robert was excellent company, infinitely more worldly and knowledgeable than we boys, and anyway, it was a pleasure just to listen to the sound of his voice.

At a certain point though Robert suddenly became very formal and drew himself up and literally announced (he was after all an Announcer), that he was exceedingly pleased to have been accepted by us and welcomed into our company because he was, after all, Gay. This proved to be quite a conversation stopper. Al was clearly embarrassed, mumbled something about it surely being just a fad, and got up and walked off into the bush. Lachlan didn't know what to say, other than, well mate, that's good for you. I couldn't really think of anything to add to that.

We took Robert back to his hotel. There was a rugby league test match being played between Australia and England starting around midnight, as it was an afternoon game in England. Lachlan asked Robert could we watch it on the television in his hotel room, and he let us, happily putting up with our enthusiasm for this sporting event in which he had no interest whatsoever until the early hours. Without a doubt Robert was, Lachlan observed on our way back to the coast, a real good bloke, even if he was a poofter.

It was proving to be quite a Queer journey, not that I had even the slightest understanding of the concept of Queer at the time. We continued our way up the coast, spending a bit of time hanging out in the rainforests around Mullumbimby, staying in a caravan for a few days on the beach at Byron, and finally ending up at Noosa Heads, at the house of two blokes we knew, Hodgson, usually referred to simply as simply as H, and Roy, whose name was actually Gary. We stayed for a couple weeks and then headed back south, stopping again at Big Hill and treating Robert to another day at the seaside. I remember sitting with him on the grassy rise at the back of the beach and complaining about the fact that my life didn't seem to be going anywhere. All the same, he observed, surveying the long empty stretch of sand and the dazzling blue ocean, this isn't exactly the life of a bank clerk you're leading.

5

So now it was two years later and I still hadn't taken a job in a bank.

It was the holiday season so the traffic was light even though it was mid-morning, and it didn't take us long to get through the city and over the Harbour Bridge. Gordie rummaged through the box of cassette tapes I'd made for the journey, pulling out one that started with two songs by the Teenage Radio Stars that I'd gotten off a compilation album of various Melbourne punk bands called *Lethal Weapons*, a particularly striking record pressed on white vinyl with a lurid painting of a handgun and a pool of blood on the sleeve. On the rest of the tape was The Saints' *Know Your Product*, which commenced with the punishing brass line of the title song. Gordie pushed the tape into the dashboard cassette deck and turned up the volume and gave me the smirking grin he used whenever he was pleased with himself and the situation. I was happy too, it was a good choice, great driving music.

By now numerous trips up the coast had followed our journey to Noosa Heads two years earlier. Whenever we had a few days here or a week or two there, we would head off for somewhere along the north coast, though never again getting as far as the Queensland border. Occasionally, particularly in winter, we'd go inland instead, to Bathurst or Orange or to the Snowy Mountains. Sometimes we'd take two cars, sometimes only one. The composition of the travelling groups varied, but there was always a solid core of myself, Lachlan and, or, Al. This would then be supplemented by the presence of one or more of a group that included Gordie, Kevin, Pazza, Plushie and the only woman in our circle, Silvana, or Silvie. She was the only girl we knew who didn't act like a girl.

When *Know Your Product* ended Gordie turned the tape over. *Never Mind the Bollocks Here's the Sex Pistols* was on the other side. He grinned again; 'God Save the Queen' was more or less his signature tune. We bypassed Newcastle to the sound of 'Holidays in the Sun' and 'Anarchy in the UK' and 'Pretty Vacant', and then bypassed our regular stomping grounds as the kilometres of the afternoon faded to vanishing point in the rear view mirror. We stopped to fill up at a petrol station near Grafton and ate hamburgers and chips in the café and then got back into the Ford and drove for another couple of hours. By this time it was getting late, it had been dark for a while, so I pulled into a rest area off the highway at the top of a pass west of Byron Bay. There was no infrastructure of any kind, just a flat space of gravelly dirt for cars or trucks to stop for a rest, and to us it seemed the ideal space to spend the night.

Despite my aversion to all-night travel, over the past couple of years we had developed a habit of doing exactly that, driving wide-awake through the dark hours to Big Hill or Crescent Head after having taken tabs of acid, on which it was of course impossible to sleep. Generally, we'd supplement the acid with a bottle of bourbon, mixing it with coke and passing it around the car as we drove, laughing and talking rubbish and invariably managing to knock off the whole bottle before the sky got light. But this time there was none of this recreational foolishness, because we wanted to get to Brisbane as quickly as we could.

We got out our sleeping bags and unrolled them on the ground next to the car. Thousands of stars twinkled overhead, only dimming as the intermittent headlights of passing cars and trucks briefly lit up the rock wall to our left. We were pretty tired after a day of driving in the summer heat and I dropped off to sleep almost straight away, stirring only occasionally at the rumble of a semi-trailer negotiating the crest of the hill.

What really strikes me now when I think about this scene is how utterly fearless we were. A book that had I had become obsessed with two or three years earlier was *The Forgotten Soldier*, a memoir of the war against the Soviet Union by a young Alsatian-German, Guy Sajer. An early passage describes the shock and bewilderment that Sajer and his young comrades feel when, late in the evening, their Sergeant calls a halt to their first day's march into the Ukraine and orders them to lie down on the ground and sleep. All well brought up German boys, they can barely comprehend that they are expected to simply spend the night in the open. It's the first time any of them have ever experienced such barbarism.

But to us it seemed the most ordinary thing in the world to be lying next to the highway on the open ground under the night sky. We weren't engaged in a war I suppose, and anyway, we were next to our car, the ultimate symbol of both sovereignty and security for a young man in our society. And anyway, what dangers did we face? No one would try to rob us because there were three of us. And as it was, we had little to steal. We had no mobile phones or ipods or laptops; they hadn't been invented yet and nobody had any idea that within barely a decade it would be impossible to be happy without the ability to access, process, create or transfer information every minute of the day. We had no cards either, credit cards were unobtainable for young itinerants like us while ATMs had only appeared in Australia a few years earlier and hardly anyone used them, especially no-hopers like us. If you wanted money you had to take your passbook to the bank and ask for it from the teller. So, all we had was some cash in our pockets. So, the only real threat was a truck running off the road and squashing us, and this was probably unlikely.

6

In the morning we crossed into Queensland and stopped at Burleigh Heads and jumped out of the car and ran into the surf. The water was like a luke-warm bath and we laughed and mucked around in the waves for a while. Then we got back into the car and drove up to Brisbane and across the Story Bridge and went on past the airport to the north suburban coast.

Glen and Louise lived in Scarborough, a peninsular-like extension of the better-known suburb of Redcliffe. There was an old concrete seawall along the ocean and the place had a quiet and overlooked feel to it, something like a rundown Victorian seaside town. Not that I actually knew anything about such towns, I'd never been to England, I'd never been anywhere really, but I'd read about them and seen them on television. No doubt Brisbane's Scarborough had been named after the archetypal Victorian seaside town of the same name on the Yorkshire coast (which I would visit a couple of times some ten to twenty years later, with my partner Fiona, whose family was from Yorkshire), but this was a place that, at this point in my life, I'd never heard of.

It was a humid Queensland morning but the sea air was pleasant and after a bit of driving around in circles we found Glen's street. I wasn't really looking forward to seeing him: he was Al's friend but I found him pretty annoying: he was constantly out of it and often didn't have much to say, and on the odd occasions when he did, he invariably spoke in short, slow, enigmatic or just plain asinine sentences. His eyelids were permanently droopy and his tired smile revealed an uneven string of yellow, rotten-looking junkie teeth. Louise on the other hand – skinny, freckly and a bit skittish – I quite liked.

And it was Louise who greeted us at the screen door of the small weath-erboard house with the news that Glen wasn't there, nor were Lachlan or

Al. They'd left a few days earlier for a painting job at Moranbah in Central Queensland. Louise ushered us in and put the kettle on and we sat down at the wooden kitchen table. It was mid-morning by this point and we'd had no breakfast, so tea would be more than welcome, along with the pieces of toast Louise began to pile on a plate in the middle of the table. She poured us each a mug of tea and I immediately began to guzzle mine when suddenly, like a sweaty, shirtless apparition, Alka, drawn no doubt by the prospect of food and drink which he'd not had to provide for himself, appeared from the spare room at the back of the house in which he had no doubt been dozing.

Alka had been left behind to wait for us. His name was Matt Riles, but he'd acquired the moniker Alka because of the tight brown ringlets covering his scalp, which some smartarse so-called friend had compared to Alka Seltzer, an antacid relentlessly marketed on TV throughout the 1970s. His wardrobe was predominantly white, pretty much at odds with everyone else in those days, and he stood before us now wearing nothing other than a slightly embarrassed grin and a pair of white shorts, the well-cut sort you found in the casual-wear section of a department store. He never shopped for his own clothes, his aunt ('Auntie' as he always called her) with whom he lived and into whose care he'd been entrusted as a boy always bought them for him. So he was never less than immaculately dressed and groomed and therefore completely at odds with the rest of us; indeed, every time my mother saw him she'd make some remark about how impressed she was by the way Auntie 'kept him'.

Alka had never had a job, a psychiatrist had been medicating him for years and he received Sickness Benefits payments from the Department of Social Security. Yet despite the fact that he was as mad as a meataxe as the saying went, Alka could still be surprisingly good company a lot of the time, aside from the mood swings which would reduce him to tears. Alka had been left in Scarborough for two reasons: one, because he was no manual worker, he was no worker of any kind, and two, because the bench seat of Al's panel van could only accommodate three people. So the plan, much no doubt to Louise's relief (given that she had been forced to adopt Auntie's role by default), was that Gordie and Kevin and I should collect Alka and follow the other three up to Moranbah. Glen had confirmed the arrangements in a phone call (from a public phone box of course) to Louise after he arrived; there was, he had said, plenty of work up there for all of us.

So, where the fuck was Moranbah? Louise got up from the table and pulled a road map of Queensland from one of the kitchen cabinet's wooden drawers and spread it out on the table. The rest of us gathered around it cradling our mugs of tea. Moranbah was one thousand, one hundred and two kilometers away to the north, a couple of hours drive inland from the coast in the middle of the Bowen Basin, a coal mining region that covered an area the size of Tasmania. Glen, who was a house painter, had heard through a contractor about a job painting a primary school under construction there. Al and Glen had worked together in Sydney painting and decorating for an Eastern Suburbs real estate agency, before Glen and Louise had moved back to Brisbane, which is where Louise was originally from. Al hadn't done an apprenticeship in painting but he'd had a lot of experience and was working at getting a license as a builder. Lachlan meanwhile liked to think of himself as an intellectual, but as a man of the people he also liked to have a go at manual work if it was presented to him.

Moranbah sounded familiar, and I remembered that a few years earlier the town had featured in an episode of the ABC's *Four Corners* program, in which Paul Lyneham exposed the extent to which the Queensland Government was letting an American multinational exploit Australia's coal resources, while he simultaneously skewered the despicable and corrupt Premier Joh Bjelke-Petersen over the question of conflict of interest, by showing how he owned shares in another mining company that was tendering to supply coal to a government-owned power station. You … you … you … people, Bjelke-Petersen had blustered in answer to Lyneham's questions, would you want to have a Premier … or a … or a … leader who had never owned anything … never achieved anything … is … is that what you want? It was great current affairs television, and for me, who liked to think of himself as a Marxist (even though I didn't actually know much about Marxism), it had been an outstanding depiction of the evils of capitalism.

Ok Alka, said Gordie as he drained his mug of tea and demonstratively plonked it back down on the table, go and pack your bag. We're goin'.

7

Louise put together some sandwiches for us to take for lunch. We made our way across the northern suburbs of Brisbane to the Bruce Highway, and by early afternoon we were at Gympie. To me the name sounded quintessentially 'Queensland'. We stopped in the middle of town and got out of the car and sat in the park under the shade of an old jacaranda and ate our sandwiches and then had a look around the shops. I flicked through a pile of worn out books in a wire basket outside a secondhand shop. There was nothing very interesting, mostly just science fiction, Robert E. Heinlein and Michael Moorcock, fat old paperbacks with spines that had been broken and re-broken a thousand times, the pages all brown and dried up. Nobody was interested in these books anymore; it seemed like the Queensland climate would eat them up long before anybody tried to read them again. We went into the supermarket and bought some cigarettes and some packets of chips and bottles of Coke.

It was hot and sunny and the entire population of the town appeared to be dressed in shorts and t-shirts, so we didn't look out of place. I suggested that we go for a swim at the local swimming pool, there had to be one in a town this size after all, and there was general though not enthusiastic agreement that this was a reasonable idea. Actually, Kevin and I had spent an afternoon at a municipal pool somewhere in south Brisbane about ten years earlier. Kevin and his mother and sister always stayed with an aunt for a couple of weeks of the summer holidays at Mt. Gravatt, and one year we went on a holiday to Queensland too, my father driving my mother and I up to Brisbane and the Gold Coast in our Kingswood. Kevin was my closest friend at school, and his mother and my mother were friends as well, so they organised for us to spend a day together at a swimming centre. It was a beautiful old stone place, the product perhaps of a Depression-era work-creation project. It had a water slide and we had a carefree summer's afternoon frolicking about. Ten years later this childhood memory was fuelling my desire for a plunge into what would no doubt be an over-chlorinated, over-crowded local council pool. We got back into the car and drove around, with me hoping that we'd find a pool in one of the nearby streets. I don't know why I didn't just ask someone for directions, but after ten minutes or so of driving and looking we'd had no sightings whatsoever of any pools, municipal or otherwise, and so Gordie persuaded me to let go of the idea. I turned the Ford around and we headed back to the highway.

Just like the day before, we drove north all through the afternoon, the major differences being Alka sitting in the back seat and the increasing enormity of the Queensland landscape. At one point we crested a hill, or maybe it was a small mountain, and to the northwest an unbroken expanse of scrubby green trees looked to extend to infinity. Fucken hell, Gordie exclaimed, and we all laughed at the absurdity of the sight, a landscape that said to us that we were utterly irrelevant. We passed by Maryborough and the turnoff to Hervey Bay and then Gin Gin and the road to Bundaberg. I was thinking that we could make a detour to Bundaberg and have a look at the place. I only knew two things about it, one being that it was where Bert Hinkler the aviator was from. Hinkler was famous for his solo flights, he'd been the first man to fly non-stop from Sydney to Bundaberg and from London to Riga. Granted, not the most important or influential of routes, but still he was an Aussie and he'd been famous and anyway I liked his name, Bert, a name that to me signified old men who knew what they were doing. And the other piece of information I possessed, along with pretty much everybody else, was that they made rum in Bundaberg. I felt quite drawn to the place, but again, neither Gordie nor Kevin nor Alka were too interested, even despite the lure of the rum, for which huge sickly yellow advertising billboards had begun to line the road over the previous few kilometres.

A thin sheet of light grey cloud was slowly covering the blue sky. Another reason I'd wanted to divert to Bundaberg was that I was feeling as if I needed a rest. But Gordie insisted we should continue on to Gladstone, another 150 kilometres away. Apparently a bloke he knew from the railway workshops had spent a few months there working on the construction of an aluminium smelter. It was a wild place, so he said, a real *rage*. We should stop at Gladstone, Gordie went on, and go to a pub and have a few beers. Kevin and Alka, who didn't really have any opinions as to what we should do or how we should do it, agreed with him. So Gladstone it was. What did I care if I had to drive another 150 kilometres? I'd just driven one and a half thousand in the previous day and a half.

8

We parked the car in the middle of Gladstone above the docks and went into the nearest pub. It was about five in the afternoon and the place was packed. Bloodshot-eyed sun-browned men in dirty overalls or King Gee shorts and shirts lined the bar, many with scratched and battered hard-hats hanging from their belts. Condensation sweated down the sides of the glasses of cold beer they all maneuvered as they nodded in agreement with each other's conversational gambits. Other groups of similarly dressed blokes stood around high tables sucking in lungfulls of smoke from adroitly handled cigarettes. It was the after work rush hour and we were right in the middle of it.

I elbowed my way through to the bar and waited for a barmaid to notice me. After a couple of minutes a middle-aged woman with a plain, round face asked was I right mate? Four schooners of XXXX please I answered, realising my appalling error even before the words were completely out of my mouth. She made no reply but simply gave me a hostile glare while the men standing on either side of me momentarily turned away from their discussions to look me up and down dismissively before shifting their atten-tion back to their mates and their beers. Sorry, I said, um, I meant four pots. The barmaid harrumphed and then took her time filling the glasses. I handed over my two dollars and she turned without comment to ring up the till. I picked up the four beers together, one of many skills I'd devel-oped behind the bar myself, and carried them over to our table by the wall.

It had been thirsty work, driving all day through the Queensland heat, more than enough to warrant a line in a VB advertisement, and I downed my pot in a couple of minutes. Not that there was any Victoria Bitter avail-able, nor Tooheys nor Reschs or anything else pitifully southern, just the ubiquitous XXXX, also advertised, like Bundaberg Rum, via a dazzling palette of red and yellow. Yellow, it seemed, was the colour of the hangover in Queensland. Actually, I'd never liked XXXX very much. On my first trip to Queensland as a child, the logo (which seemed to be everywhere I looked), featuring a strange little caricature of a man wearing a boater emblazoned with the four Xs, had really disturbed me. He had a wizened face that seemed to my young mind the embodiment of evil (as I'm sure he was for legions of Queensland housewives), but when I tried to tell my father about this he just laughed it off. Now, as a grown up beer drinker, I wasn't that keen on the taste either, it was too thin and too sweet. But they said it went well with the heat.

Gordie went to the bar next and came back and planted his round on the table. He, on the other hand, seemed as happy as a pig in shit: for him drinking XXXX was the very embodiment of *raging*. Back home in Sydney he and his drug dealer mates would often buy a case of XXXX whenever they felt like an impromptu party. Now, not only was he drinking XXXX, he was actually drinking it in Queensland, the semi-mythical land of real men and tough but compliant sheilas which he'd been dreaming of for years and was finally experiencing first hand. Not that there were many sheilas in this pub aside from those behind the bar. Tradesmen and labourers surrounded us because construction work on the aluminium smelter was at its peak and there were a couple of thousand workers in the town employed directly or indirectly on the project. In the 1950s Conzinc Rio Tinto had begun mining bauxite at Weipa on Cape York, after the Queensland Government and police had expelled the traditional owners from the area for them. The subsequent development of the Bowen Basin coal mines (to which we were headed), had then made the economics of a coal fired power station in the Gladstone region (paid for by the Queensland and Federal Governments), both viable and attractive to a multinational company interested in building one of the world's biggest aluminum smelters, an installation which would suck up a staggering amount of electricity. Work on the smelter had been going on for more than a year now, and although we didn't realise it, here in this pub in Gladstone we'd stumbled right into the great consolidation of the minerals export boom that had originally begun during the 1960s. Now this boom was settling down into a pattern of more or less constant expansion that would continue for decades, a particular kind of nation building in which even we would get to play our own insignificant part.

We finished Gordie's round and then Kevin had his shout and then Alka, and after four middies – sorry, pots, it had been a long day – I was starting to feel a bit pissed. By now it was after 7pm and there was no sign of the boisterous pub atmosphere surrounding us settling down. If anything, it was getting more raucous as everyone became increasingly well-oiled. I realised we only had two options, to keep drinking and get absolutely hammered and then find somewhere to spend the night in Gladstone, or to move on. I knew Rockhampton was only about one hundred kilometres away, so I suggested that we get back in the car and drive up there, then have something to eat and find somewhere to sleep. Surprisingly, Gordie agreed, and even more surprisingly, he asked if he could drive. Tired as I was, I agreed. Half an hour later, as he weaved around on the dark highway behind the enormous cattle truck he was trying to overtake, I was regretting the ease with which I'd relinquished control of my vehicle. The road seemed an endless stream of bends, a new one appearing every time Gordie attempted to pull out, only to have to pull back in again as a glaring flash of oncoming headlights leapt out of the blackness ahead accompanied by the manic blast of an approaching horn which would invariably set off another round of mournful bellowing from the cows in the back of the truck.

But eventually we got past the truck, leaving the cows and their most likely unpleasant fate far behind. It was around 9pm by the time we reached Rockhampton and pulled into the parking lot of the local Pizza Hut. We went in and sat down. There weren't many customers this late on what was a Wednesday night, though in any case the days of the week were pretty much irrelevant to us. We ordered four large pizzas, accompanied by the ubiquitous XXXX. The young waitress was surprisingly pleasant, given how smelly and dirty we were. Alka found a strange object in his pizza, a little ball of some clear plasticky substance, silicone maybe, kind of like translucent snot. Gordie pushed it around on the table with his finger for a while and then flicked it at Kevin, who told him to get fucked.

We finished the pizzas and the beer and paid the bill and left a small tip – a quite remarkable act for us – and went out and got into the car and plunged into the back streets in search of a primary school. We found one within a few minutes and drove in and parked and got out our sleeping bags and set them down on the wooden boards of the verandah of the main classroom building. Within minutes I was sound asleep.

9

The next morning I woke up in the tropics. I looked at my watch and it was just before 8am, it must have already been light for a couple of hours but I'd been so tired I'd hardly stirred all night. I sat up and looked around. Alka was propped on his elbows across from me, smiling broadly. I smiled back.

There was a homely, friendly smell to the timbers of the school building. Next to the three or four steps down from the verandah was a hibiscus with big orange-red flowers, and further towards the street in the midst of a lush deep green lawn there was a group of Alexander palms. The sky was grey and low and the air damp, but there'd been no rain. The day seemed somehow warm and cool at the same time.

It was the school holidays, so we didn't need to worry about teachers and kids turning up at any moment, but still, a caretaker or somebody might be along soon, so we needed to skedaddle. Gordie was awake but Kevin, whose anti-psychotic medication made him drowsy, was always hard to rouse in the morning. Alka gave his shoulder a shake. Come on Kev, wake up mate.

I jumped off the verandah and went over to the Ford and opened the tailgate and threw in my sleeping bag. Then I went around and opened the driver's door to pull the latch that released the bonnet catch, so that I could check the oil and the water after such a long drive. I went to the front of the car and felt around for the catch and found it and pulled it back and tilted the heavy sheet of metal up on its hinges. I took off the radiator cap and looked inside. The pipe was dry, the radiator definitely needed water, and I went back around to get the jerry can. Gordie was standing next to the verandah pissing, a thick pale stream of urine squirting onto the grass in front of him. I looked at his squat pink cock in his right hand and I remembered standing at a school assembly six or seven years earlier and trying to pay attention to whatever it was our famous communist Headmistress was going on about while he bragged to me about having got a Greek girl from our year called Elena to suck him off. Did you hear what Elena said about me, he asked? No, I hadn't. She said I've got an eight-inch dick. She did? Yeah, she did. I smiled to myself while Gordie, oblivious to the caprices of my memory, continued pissing and looking at me blankly through the thick lenses of his glasses. I pulled out the jerry can and went back around to the front of the car and upended it so that a gush of liquid gurgled down into the throat of the radiator. Then I pulled out the oil stick and wiped the runny black excess on my fingers and then plunged it back into the sheath. I pulled it out again and looked at the level. It was fine, so I put it back in. Then I bent down and wiped my oily fingers on the grass. You're a polluter, Kevin said, watching me from the verandah.

I took the jerry can back around to the rear of the car and stowed it away. Kevin was still stuffing around on the verandah rolling up his sleeping bag while Alka sat on the steps smoking a cigarette. I walked across the grass and looked up and down the street. We were about a kilometre north of the latitude line marking the Tropic of Capricorn, but I knew that because the tilt on the earth's axis wasn't fixed but rather was in a constant slow movement, the line delineating the tropics was slowly moving as well and so the tropics were shrinking in each direction by about 15 metres a year. So, in 70 years the spot on which I was standing wouldn't be in the tropics anymore. If I were still alive then I'd be Aunt Millie's age. I looked up and down the street once more, at the strip of asphalt running down the middle and at the gravelly dirt on either side of the street and at the light poles and the wooden houses on stilts opposite. None of it was really solid and fixed in place, it just looked like it was.

10

The Horror Stretch was next, two hundred and fifty kilometres of empty road from Marlborough – just to the north of Rockhampton – to Sarina, south of Mackay. It was famous for gruesome murders, shootings, assaults and head on collisions. The latter were attributed to the monotony of the scrubby, miserable landscape, but maybe some of the other acts of random violence could be put down to this cause too. Gordie had been talking up the prospect of our meeting with the Horror Stretch all the previous afternoon, elaborating and extending on the various hysterical anecdotes he'd picked up from his North Queensland contacts.

A few kilometres further on from Rockhampton we came to a place called The Caves. There were some limestone caves just off the highway, the Mount Etna Caves, named for the Sicilian volcano that had erupted and stopped the Carthaginians capturing Syracuse from the Greeks in 396 BC. Etna had been periodically erupting ever since, and I was sure neither the geography nor the history of this geologically quiet part of Central Queensland had anything at all in common with the east coast of Sicily. Still, some conquering European had seen fit to bestow this exotic name upon the place.

I was really keen to go through one of the caves, and for once I didn't ask for opinions, I just acted. I pulled off the highway and followed a short road up to a car park in front of a cliff wall. I loved caves. One of my earliest memories was of my father carrying me on his shoulders through the subterranean labyrinth of the Jenolan Caves in the Blue Mountains when I must have only been about three or four. I could still see the stalactites and stalagmites glistening against the darkness in the stark electric light. And just six months ago Silvana had taken Al and myself to visit a friend of hers who was working as a park ranger at a group of limestone caves called Yarangobilly, in the Snowy Mountains. It had been mid-winter, and we'd stayed for a few days, sleeping on the floor in front of a big fire in the ranger's house, an old Federation mansion. At night, after the tourists had left, he'd take us into the caves and we'd smoke joints and marvel at the intricacies of nature and the Universe and then walk back through the snow to the house.

I parked the car and we got out. Ferns hung from cracks and crevices in the overhanging granite walls and thin mountain pines gave off a cool morning scent under the light grey sky. It was wonderful, but a sign told us that the caves didn't open until midday, and it was only about 9am. Another sign said that the caves were the roosting place of most the Australian population of the Small Bent-Winged Bat, as well as a population of Ghost Bats. Perhaps an additional reason I wanted to stop at the caves was because, unlike Gordie, who seemed to relish the prospect, the idea of traversing the Horror Stretch made me a little nervous. But there wasn't much chance of me convincing him that we should wait around for three hours until the caves opened. And neither Kevin's nor Alka's opinions could ever really be trusted because of the amount of psychotropic medications they were on, so I didn't even bother with them. There wasn't even a café for us to get breakfast, so we got back into the car and drove away towards the Horror Stretch. Ghost Bats: it didn't seem like a very good omen.

We stopped at a service station in Marlborough and filled the Ford up with petrol and then went to the café. One of the key Horror Stretch scenarios concerned travelers running out of fuel somewhere along the way and then being raped and mutilated and decapitated by persons unknown. We ordered pots of tea and raisin toast and talked through the possibilities, like, what if the car overheated? Or, what if we got a flat tyre? We had plenty of water and a good spare, I declared, trying to convince myself as much as anyone else that there was nothing to worry about. What if we get two flat tyres, asked Alka, unhelpfully. Then we're fucked, smirked Gordie, and chuckled evilly. I finished my tea and toast and went to the toilet for a piss, then went out to the car to check the water again, just in case. The radiator cap had cooled enough for me to remove it and have a look, but the water level was fine. The other three dawdled out of the café a little while later. We got into the car and Gordie fished around in his bag and pulled out a knife, a medium-sized hunting knife with an angry-looking pointy tip. Where the fuck did you get that, I asked? She's a fucken' beaut, isn't she, he said. I looked over to the petrol station and through the glass windows of the front wall to the fat, balding manager behind the counter who was looking directly back at Gordie as he waved his blade around in the front seat. For fuck's sake put it away, I said. He did, with a final flourish. Nobody's gunna fuck with me, he said, looking at each of us in turn.

But actually, there proved to be nothing too horrible about the Horror Stretch. No one tried to 'fuck' with Gordie or indeed with any of us. We didn't break down or run off the road and I managed to avoid colliding head on with any of the cars and trucks we passed, of which there were a lot more than I'd expected. Boredom was the only notable issue, the landscape was indeed monotonous, but in the company of three ratbags and with the Sex Pistols blasting on the car stereo even this wasn't too much of a problem.

Nonetheless it *was* quite boring, the world outside the windscreen, with the only alleviation of note provided by an abandoned petrol station somewhere along the way, all shot full of holes by trigger-happy passersby. It was the most depressing of ruins, all alone in a sparse terrain, a jumble of tin and fibro and broken glass and peeling paint, a splotch of ephemeral Australiana ruined before it had even managed to establish itself. Of course, I was looking at everything through a particular lens, and Indigenous Australians would no doubt have seen the landscape very differently to me, finding a wealth of detail to appreciate where for me there was only incomprehension. Then again, maybe all the place would have been for them now was a Horror Stretch as well, given the unknown number of Aborigines murdered along the way by police and colonists during the nineteenth and twentieth centuries. Maybe there really are places that are simply just bad, where bad things happen and then just perpetuate themselves. But it was hard to know, because so many bad things had already been said about this place in advance that it was impossible to approach it with an open mind.

Anyway, I forgot all about the Horror Stretch as a few hours later we slid down the hill towards Sarina, a surprisingly green and pleasant town surrounded by cane fields. We stopped at a roadside stall and bought some bananas, and then turned off the Bruce Highway and drove along a back road through farmland that took us up to the Peak Downs Highway, which connected the Bowen Basin to the coast. We turned onto the highway. A sign said that Moranbah was 183 kilometres away.

11

We were passing through farmland, mostly big reassuring paddocks of sugar cane, but as we headed inland the arable land again morphed into the gnarly scrub that seemed to cover most of inland Queensland. It would only take another couple of hours to get there; there wasn't too much traffic, it was the middle of the day and we were outside the morning and afternoon commute periods.

Commute seemed an apposite word, because Moranbah, as we approached the outskirts, looked like nothing so much as a modern suburb that some giant hand had picked up from a coastal city and dumped in the middle of the bush. Suddenly there were neat timber and fibro homes everywhere: single or double fronted with verandahs and green lawns that were obviously no stranger to either sprinkler or Victa, while kerbed and guttered cul de sacs dotted with more houses arced off the main street in both directions. I pulled the car into the parking lot of the commercial centre of the town: a brick veneer terrace of shops and services that looked just like your average suburban cluster: a post office, a couple of banks, a butcher's, a baker's, a fish n' chip shop (even though we were two hundred kilometres from the sea), a take-away, a newsagent and a small supermarket. The only thing missing was a video shop, because hardly anyone was watching videos yet, not even on Beta.

We were hungry, we hadn't had anything to eat since breakfast on the other side of the Horror Stretch, and so we ordered hamburgers and chips in the take-away. The Coal Country Caravan Park, according to the woman who served us the food, was only a few minutes away, towards the western side of town. There was something like a sigh of resignation in her voice as she gave me the directions, a quality that made its presence known even within her languid Queensland drawl, as if she'd been asked this question too many times by scruffy young men who needed a shower. After we'd used the last of our chips to mop up the puddles of barbeque sauce and egg yolk the hamburgers had left on our plates, we went back out to the car and drove over to the caravan park.

As the name Coal Country indicated – rather than something like Golden Sands or Mermaid's Haven – it was the sort of caravan park you lived in rather than visited on your annual holidays. Rows of tightly packed, multi-berth aluminum vans with tent-like canvas annexes lined the grid of gravel paths that spread out from the entrance. Some had television aerials sprouting from their roofs, others had a barbeque set up next to the annex, and some, domiciles of the park elite, had both. The van we were in search of possessed neither, but we found it easily enough because it was the only caravan in the park with a Great Dane in the annex. Tess, Lachlan's dog, recognised us even before we saw her, and she jumped up and loped out to greet us, all muscle and sinew and the size of a small pony. She butted her human-sized head up against me and I gave the back of her neck a big scratch and then ran my hand over her back and slapped her rump a couple of times. It was good to see her. Then she opened her mouth and yawned and sauntered back into the annex.

It was getting towards late afternoon, but neither Lachlan nor Al nor Glen was around, they obviously weren't back from work yet. The caravan wasn't locked so we let ourselves in. There were bunks for four inside plus a double bed, so if a couple of us slept on the annex floor there would be room enough. Gordie found some tea in the cupboard above the small sink and filled up the electric kettle with water to make a pot. I went back to get the car from where we'd left it at the entrance. I considered calling into the park office to make our presence legal, but I decided it could wait until later. By the time I parked the Ford in the allotted space, Gordie was pouring the tea.

There was a portable picnic table set up in the annex and so we sat down around it on fold-up patio chairs, the type that were made out of crosshatched strips of nylon mesh fabric and aluminium frames with wooden armrests. It seemed the height of luxury after a few days in the car and we sipped the hot milky tea sweetened with multiple spoonfulls of sugar, dunking the scotch finger biscuits we'd also found in the cupboard and sweating blithely in the enfolding humidity as we chuckled over a recapitulation of our trip. Tess lay on the ground next to us, stirring every now and then and shifting her paws around in dreamy pursuit of bears and boars in cold north European forests. It was hot and airless under the canvas. A storm seemed to be brewing.

12

There was only ever going to be one course of action after we all finally met up: we would go to the pub. A couple of hours later I was at the bar of the Black Nugget Hotel buying a round of XXXX. Gordie had come with me to help with the carry, as picking up seven glasses of beer was beyond even my level of service industry dexterity. There was a big television set on a shelf above the bottles of spirits, and as the surly, flat-faced, redheaded female Queenslander pulled our beers an advertisement was trumpeting the approach of Australia Day, which was less than 48 hours away. In those days this was an occasion about which your average Aussie couldn't really give a fuck, only dickheads went round waving the flag, and the ad was obviously intended to help promote the regrowth of a bit of backbone in a society that was perceived to be going to the dogs: One Nation – One Future, shouted a bold-fonted green and gold graphic over a particularly strident rendition of *Advance Australia Fair* in a manner that seemed to anticipate all sorts of unpleasant developments. No Future responded Gordie, mimicking Johnny Rotten's diction and then following it with his self-satisfied chuckle. I laughed too; it was as funny as it was obvious.

It was a mid-week night but the pub was full of people, mostly men, getting stuck into all the usual pub activities: playing pool, darts, even quoits in one corner, watching harness racing on television, eating steak and chips, shouting conversational gambits at each other, or just listening to *Evie* parts one, two and three on the jukebox, though in the end all of us were united as one via the fact that everyone, no matter what their temporary diversions, was also drinking beer and smoking cigarettes. Actually I didn't really smoke, just the odd one now and then, mostly when I was drunk, but the excitement of the moment must have gotten to me because

I'd bludged a Benson and Hedges off Kevin and was really enjoying suck-ing the toxins into my lungs. Gordie and I plonked the beers down in the middle of the table and I removed the smoldering ciggie from between my lips for a moment before putting it back and taking a drag, exhaling slowly as I sat back down. We each picked up a glass and clinked them together over the centre of the table and someone said Cheers or There Ya Go or something similar. All around us the life of the town was being played out. Once upon a time the social centre of a remote rural locality like Moranbah might have been the church, or the school of arts, but not any more. Not that there was actually anything remote now about an airstrip and high-way-connected place like Moranbah, apart that is from its location on the map.

It was good to see Lachlan and Albert. Glen I could have done without, but Al really liked him, and anyway, it was his connections that were respon-sible for us being there, so I supposed I had to give credit where it was due. Lachlan was full of enthusiasm for the work they were now undertaking, painting a new primary school the Queensland Government had just built to help instruct the ever-growing pool of children in the town. Possessed of an artistic temperament, Lachlan never saw his own experience of the actual labour that most people were compelled to perform for their daily bread as any sort of displeasing necessity. Rather, working in order to be paid was an activity he only ever imagined as transitory, and it excited him in the way a bored person might suddenly become enamoured of a new hobby. He'd been painting landscapes and portraits for years, and our art class at school had often been dominated by arguments between him and our teacher over issues to do with Realism and representation, arguments that only continued and became more longwinded when sometimes we'd go out drinking with the teacher on Friday nights after school. Lachlan was no Expressionist, for him the object painted had to look more or less like its analogue in the real world, and so maybe this is why he saw industrial painting, the painting of houses and buildings, as some sort of massively expanded version of his creative work on canvas. He'd had no training as a housepainter of course; he only knew what he'd picked up from Al, as well as whatever ineffable particulars he had apparently imbibed via osmosis from his affinity for paint. That said, he was really enjoying the work, and urged me to sign on too. It seemed like a good idea.

When the pub closed at 11pm we stumbled out into the humid night and made our way back to the caravan park. The storm that had formed up earlier had passed, the sky was clear now and big puddles of water reflected some of the bright stars hanging overhead in the velvety black sky. It was quite dark, there weren't many streetlights, but it was only a few hundred metres from the pub to the caravan park and anyway there was no danger of becoming lost because it was a path that was well-worn, not just by Lachlan and Al and Glen but, it seemed, by a large segment of the park population, and we formed part of what was more or less a drunken procession through the centre of town. Impromptu as it was, it was also obvious that the rowdy parade was a regular evening feature.

When we got back to the caravan Al ticked me off once again for taking the allotted parking spot and so forcing him to squeeze his Holden panel van into the space between the front of the van and the gravel pathway. First come first serve I said, to which he said that's exactly what he meant. Bad luck, I said, and laughed. Then Lachlan, who'd put the kettle on for a cup of tea, had a go at all of us newcomers for having eaten all the scotch finger biscuits. Bad luck, we said, and laughed. And so it went on, until Glen climbed onto the top bunk next to the kitchenette and rolled over and quite soon began to snore. It wasn't too long before the rest of us followed him into dreamland.

13

An alarm clock went off about 6.30. Al had set it but in any case I was no longer asleep; I never slept well after a night of heavy drinking, usually waking, with a dry throat and a headache, as soon as it started to get light. I looked around. Glen lolled on his bunk blinking his bulbous marsupial eyes and smiling his rotten-toothed smile as Al passed him up a mug of tea. Lachlan, who unsurprisingly had taken the double bed at the opposite end of the caravan, groaned and pulled his pillow over his head. Gordie was snoring on the bunk above me. Kevin and Alka were quiet, both still in their sleeping bags in the annex. Glen took a few sips of his tea and then slipped down and took a seat at the table, crossing his skinny white legs and lighting a cigarette, which was his idea of breakfast. I pulled myself out of bed and went over to the kitchen bench and poured a mug of tea from the pot. Al put some bread in the toaster. Lachlan sat up and shook his head and said fucken hell. Shut up you cunts, stop makin so much fucken noise, said Gordie, roused from his slumber by our inconsiderate attention to our own needs.

I had some panadeine in my bag, I suppose it was a bit of a habit but what the fuck, you could get them over the counter, so I took two and lay back down on my bunk after the other three had left, and then fell back to sleep, waking a couple of hours later in the midst of a particularly strident burst of snoring from Gordie. Codeine and paracetamol made me dream, and when consciousness intruded this time I was in the middle of a funeral. Is she your mother, someone had asked, pointing at Millie, seemingly oblivious to the fact that she was at least sixty years older than me. I didn't know what it meant, this dream. I was 21, I hadn't really been to that many funerals, although it was true I'd escorted Millie to a couple of them in the last year or so, services for family members so obscure I wasn't even that sure where they fitted into our tree. I got up and pulled on my shorts and a singlet and stepped out into the annex and Tess raised herself onto her front paws to say good morning, so I nodded at her. Kevin and Alka, up to their eyeballs in a mixture of alcohol and psychotropic drugs, slept on oblivious to everything around them in the real world.

I put on my thongs and got in the car and drove over to the supermarket. It was a bright sunny day and hot even though it was still only mid-morning, and as I pulled off my sunglasses the cool breeze from the fan mounted on the wall behind the register hit me in the face. I glanced at the fruit and veggie section against the far wall, but it was a depressing experience: a few ragged lettuces, some dried-up carrots, a couple of dozen anaemic tomatoes and some tired potatoes on one shelf with some wormy-looking apples and withered oranges on the other. Curiously, given that this was the sunshine state, there was no sign of either bananas or pineapples. And the prices for the sad-looking objects that actually were present seemed at least twice what you would have paid in Sydney: the tyranny of distance was hard at work. On the other hand, the shelves were packed with an abundance of sugar and flour and spaghetti and white bread and biscuits and tea and instant coffee and chocolate and packets of chips and various other kinds of mass-produced, more easily transported provisions, the sort of stuff we pretty much lived on anyway. There was also a small deli section with lots of different types of processed pig parts, so I got some bacon and a dozen eggs then picked up a loaf of white bread and some margarine on the way out.

When I got back to the caravan the other three were awake and sitting around the kitchen table drinking tea. Good on ya mate, said Kevin, as he watched me unload the plastic supermarket bag. I frowned and passed no comment. Twenty minutes later we were tucking into bacon and eggs on toast and gulping down yet more hot tea. Dinner at the Hilton couldn't have tasted better.

It was hardly a power breakfast, but we discussed our options anyway. Our original destination, when we'd first planned the trip, had been the north,

Townsville and Cairns. Gordie knew some people in Townsville, friends of friends of his from home, and he was keen to hook up with them. They were drug dealer-types, these friends of Gordie's back in Rockdale, who I didn't actually like that much, and so I wasn't expecting much from their associates either, but still, it was a connection. North, then, was still our destination, but for the moment here we were, hundreds of kilometres from anywhere else. Gordie agreed that we should make the most of it and see if we could get some work on the primary school job as well. For Kevin and Alka on the other hand work was out totally of the question, a bit like the way it was for a caricatured beatnik character called Maynard G. Krebs in *The Many Loves of Dobie Gillis,* a television show I liked when I was young. Whenever he heard the word 'work', Maynard (played by Bob Denver who would go on to great fame as Gilligan on *Gilligan's Island)* would freak out and cry in alarm Work! Work!, as if he was having some sort of panic attack.

Gordie and I left Kevin and Alka to wash up and got in the car and drove to the primary school site on the other side of town: a group of single level timber buildings with the addition of some brick and breeze block here and there. It seemed appropriate to the town as a whole: pretty much permanent but a bit temporary at the same time and set on an arid, tree-less patch of flat ground. The building work was all finished; all that was left was the fitting out and the painting and the landscaping. I parked next to the tradies' vehicles – utes with Queensland plates – and we got out and walked over to the site office, a small demountable in the middle of a gravelly patch of dirt. The door was open and a balding fat bloke in a stained and faded blue singlet was sitting behind a desk staring at a column of figures in a ledger, a pair of reading glasses resting on the end of his snout nose. He looked about fifty years old. There was an electric fan sitting on top of the filing cabinet next to the desk, but despite its cantilevered head slowly arcing back and forth it was still stuffily hot inside the cabin. Wha'da youse want, he inquired, staring at us over his glasses as we stepped into his den, trickles of sweat running down the sides of his round, brick-red face. We told him we were looking for work. Well, yeah, there's a coupla weeks fur a

46

painta, he said, and there's a coupla weeks fur a layb'ra on the landscapin'. Three 'undred a week. Sweet, we said. Good-oh, he said, youse can start Mundy. Seven o'clock. Take these forms and fill 'em in and bring 'em back with youse then, he said, shifting his gaze back to his column of figures in a manner that indicated we were of no further interest to him whatsoever.

What should we do now, I asked Gordie when we were back out in the glare of the sunlight? Get pissed, he said, let's go the bottle'o and get a carton of XXXX.

14

Nursing a hangover as I was, the idea of spending the afternoon getting blotto again didn't really appeal, though I reasoned I could just have one or two and that I might then possibly feel better in a hair of the dog kind of way. So I stopped at the drive-in bottle shop attached to the pub. I'll get 'em said Gordie, pulling a ten-dollar note from his wallet in an apparent burst of generosity. You got the breakfast, he continued, so don't worry about it, but I'll be gettin' two fifty each off those other two cunts. I realised that he'd already factored in the detail that, as well as covering me, he'd also be drinking the lion's share of the beers and was so was hardly likely to come out of the transaction hard done by. There was a car ahead of us in the queue so he jumped out and trotted over to the counter, still wearing the red sleeveless Sex Pistols t-shirt he'd had on since we left Sydney. A couple of minutes later he was back with the carton of beer, which he affectionately cradled in his lap until we were back at the caravan.

It was a hot day, too hot in the caravan and we sat at the picnic table in the annex drinking the XXXX. Tess paced around looking at us and going to the entrance and looking up and down the gravel driveway and then coming back to pace around some more. She was obviously bored. I was bored too, for the first time since leaving home. I really wasn't in the mood for drinking more beer and the conversation wasn't going anywhere, so I finished my can and stood up and looked at her. Come on Tess, I said, we're going for a walk. Lachlan had a leash somewhere but I didn't bother to look for it because I knew she wouldn't run off, she had the temperament of a sensible human, probably more sensible than either Alka or Kevin.

We walked past the rows of caravans, most of them empty at this point in the day, although in the annexes of the odd one here and there jaded-looking young women sat in the heat with babies or young children, some of who cried out in surprise or alarm at the huge brown beast passing by, though Tess took no notice. She'd been named after Tess of the D'Urbervilles, and to me she did seem to have a similarly melancholic temperament to the character as played by Nastassja Kinski in Roman Polanski's film, which I'd seen with Silvana sometime in the middle of the previous year. Silvie had loved it and so had I even though I hadn't expected to and had only gone along to keep her company. But I hadn't been able to get the opening scene, of flower-bedecked young women dancing barefoot on deep green grass in the golden afternoon sunlight, out of my head ever since.

We passed the caravan park gate and turned onto the main road, a bland, flat strip of asphalt with suburb-like streets running off it on either side. I could hear the throb of a V8 engine approaching and I looked up as a bright orange Valiant Charger cruised pass, a young woman with long dark hair and a cigarette stuck nonchalantly between her lips behind the wheel. Her passenger, a blonde, smiled at us from behind her sunglasses and, leaning out of the open window, gave a wolf whistle, which I figured was intended for Tess rather than me. The Charger was a big, over-styled thug of a car, and Tess and I continued up the road for a couple of minutes in the wake of its exhaust before I went left down one of the side streets with Tess following me. A line of timber and fibro bungalows ran along either side of the street, each with a driveway but with no fences between the yards. I'd noticed that different parts of the town had different types of houses and that they varied a lot in terms of size and quality. These places were simple and small and must have been where the low paid unskilled workers lived. Most had kids' bicycles and toys strewn over their scraggly front lawns, and with no fences you could see into the backyards as well, some with trampolines or swing sets and, as in the caravan park, in some of the backyards young women were on their own and occupied looking after young children.

I'd been bothered by some strange feeling about the place ever since we arrived but I hadn't been able to put my finger on what it was but now suddenly the realisation came to me: there were no old people. Really, there were no grandparents, no pensioners, no senior citizens of any kind. The whole place, imitation suburb that it was, was populated exclusively by single people of working age and young nuclear families, a weird scene, like something from a science fiction film where aliens have made a copy of life on earth but haven't gotten all of the details right. Having grown up amongst elderly relatives in an extended family, this bothered me. I liked old people, they knew stuff, they knew about the world before it was the way it was now.

I was starting to feel a bit tired and was suddenly sick of walking around, the beer I'd drunk had eased my hangover but now I was getting a headache again and I felt like I needed to go to sleep for a while. The streets were in a grid pattern so I took the first left and then went left again to head back in the direction of the caravan park. Tess ran ahead of me and stopped at a small rockery in the front yard of a house, pawing at the rocks and snorting and sniffing. When I caught up I could see a big bluetongue wedged under a rock, terrified and hissing and poking its blue flickering tongue out in the hope of warding off its enormous persecutor. Come on Tess, I said, tugging at her collar, he lives here, it's his place, not yours, leave him alone. I gave another tug and she relented and we walked away. When we got back to the caravan everyone was dozing, the table covered in empty XXXX cans. It was that time of the afternoon.

15

That night we went to the pub again. It was the Friday before the long weekend so the place was even more crowded than the night before. But we managed to find a table without too much effort and commenced downing the rounds of pots. I'd slept off the remains of my hangover and so was feeling fine about repeating it.

Shouldering my way up to the bar when it was my turn I bumped into the blonde girl who'd driven past Tess and me in the Charger. I recognised her even without her sunglasses. Hey I said, I know you, which wasn't exactly true; I didn't know her, though I wanted to. Oh yeah, she said, you're the bloke with the dog. Nice dog. Thanks I said, but she's not actually my dog. Oh, that's a bummer. Not really, I said, you should see how much she eats. I couldn't afford her. But if you like I can introduce you to her owner. She laughed, and I pointed out where our table was. When I got back from the bar she and her friend with the long dark hair were already there, and Lachlan was doing his best to charm them with lovable dog stories.

Karen and Maria. They were a couple of years older than us and were nurses at the town hospital. Maria owned the Charger, and I took an immediate liking to her. Her family was Italian, the sort of cane-cutting, fruit and vegetable growing Italians who'd been in Queensland since the 1920s, and despite the two or three Aussie Italian generations behind her she still had something of the European elegance that I'd been a bit in love with ever since I'd first seen Sophia Loren in black and white on television when I was a kid. I talked to her about the car. She'd always liked cars she said, she liked working on them, changing the oil, cleaning the spark plugs, things like that. So did I, in a love-hate sort of way; I'd spent a lot of time on my back under my Ford wrestling with bolts that never wanted to come undone no matter how hard you tugged on the spanner. She'd decided to buy the Charger when she got the job at Moranbah, she said. She was from Innisfail, in the north, and was used to burning up and down the empty country roads.

Karen was talking to Lachlan about dogs, but I wasn't really listening, and eventually the conversations joined up and we drifted into table-wide group talk, which was good because I'd run out of things to say about cars. Lachlan asked about drugs. How hard was it to score here? Easy, Maria answered, we've got some barbs if you're interested. Barbiturates. Glen's droopy eyes immediately lit up. Fucken gas, he said, an antiquarian expression he used whenever he was really excited. I'd never taken barbiturates before, but lately they'd become all the rage with lots of people we knew back in Sydney, though they were pretty suspect people and I wasn't that impressed. Blue Devils, Maria continued, they're fifty cents each. Yeah, that's great Glen said. I'm in, said Gordie, smirking. Me too said Al, having taken a bit of time to think about it, as he always did. Lachlan on the other hand, despite being the most marijuana-obsessed person I'd ever met, was reticent when it came to the use of almost all other mind-altering substances apart from alcohol and so he demurred. So did Kevin and Alka, probably because they didn't want to spend the fifty cents. Ok then, Maria said, come out to the car. Well, why not I thought, when in Rome and all that.

Maria opened the passenger door of the Charger and leaned in and reached into the glove box. She was really making an impression on me: for one thing she was actually wearing a dress – a short black and white striped sleeveless shift – making her one of the few women in Moranbah not in shorts and a t-shirt. She stood up and turned around and held up a small plastic bag with a dozen or so blue pills inside. There you go, she smiled. All this was going on in plain view in the floodlit pub car park, but nobody seemed concerned. Actually, the whole exchange reminded me of an incident a few years earlier when Lachlan and Gordie and I had been looking for somewhere to pull a few cones before school, and Gordie had suggested that we just sit down with our big wooden bong on a small patch of grass in the middle of Kogarah shopping centre, just near the entrance to the railway station. The less you tried to disguise what you were doing, he argued, the less people actually noticed you. It seemed a ridiculous notion to me but we did it anyway, and strangely enough, as we sat cross-legged on the grass in the sharp morning sunlight taking turns pulling on the bong, a constant stream of briefcase and handbag wielding commuters passed by and around us without any of them giving us even the faintest of glances.

Steve Jones, the Sex Pistols' guitarist, documents a similar phenomenon. As a consequence of his dysfunctional childhood, Jones was a compulsive thief; indeed, much of the stage gear used by the Pistols in their breakthrough years had been stolen by him using what he called his 'cloak of invisibility', by which he would simply walk into a space acting as if he belonged there, pick up what he wanted and walk out without anyone paying him the slightest bit of notice. Gordie could not have known about this because it would be decades before Jones talked about it in his memoir, so he must have picked it up via some sort of punk thought transference or osmosis.

Anyway, back outside the Moranbah Black Nugget we each took a pill and handed over our fifty cents. Gordie and Glen palmed theirs and then brushed them from their hands into their mouths all in one movement, like the professionals they were. Al stared at his for awhile contemplating what could have been any number of things, then placed his on his tongue and swallowed slowly and deliberately. I held the little blue ball for a moment and then popped it into my mouth. Maria looked at me and then at the car and then at me again and said ok boys, ya wanna go for a burn? No thanks, whispered Glen, I haven't finished my beer. I was pleased about this, because I didn't see how the four of us were all going to fit onto the back seat. What about the rest of youse, asked Karen, smiling, youse game? Course we're fucken game, said Gordie.

Despite the fact that it was the size of a tank, the Charger only had two doors, and Karen laughed as she leaned the passenger seat forward to allow the three of us to pile into the back, Al in the middle because he was the skinniest, not that it mattered as it turned out because there was a lot more room than I'd expected. Maria pulled the driver's door shut and put the key into the ignition and turned it and the Charger growled into life. She revved the throttle a couple of times and then dropped the clutch and we squealed out of the car park in a spray of gravel, fishtailing onto the street as the raw power of the engine struggled to settle the big lump of metal onto a straight course. Karen whoohooed out the open window. Fucking hell said Al, chuckling and shaking his head. I couldn't have agreed more.

We hammered down the main street and within a few minutes were out in the open country as Maria talked to us over her shoulder, one hand on the wheel, her monologue affirming the obvious fact that there was fuck all to do in Moranbah and explaining how they would often drive down to the coast for a night out because it was only two hours away. Maybe we could all go there another night, but not tonight because ... because ... I don't know why ... because ... the barb was really kicking in and nothing seemed very connected to anything else anymore ... but the light in the car, the bright dark light of the night was sparkling like electricity, the way the light looked at night when you were a child, and Al was smiling like an astronaut circling the earth and Gordie was grinning out the window at the gnarled dark stumps of the trees flashing past and Maria was looking over her shoulder again at me and then ... then I was stumbling back into the dazzling white light of the inside of the pub and tripping over something and looking down I saw that it was a drunk passed out on the floor in a puddle of vomit just inside the doorway and then ... then it was the next morning and I was awake and on my bunk in the caravan.

Gordie was at the table smoking a cigarette. I sat up and stared at him and then smacked my forehead with the flat of my hand. What the fuck happened last night, I asked?

Fucked if I know, he said, smiling. Those barbs really block your memory, don't they? Fucken great eh?

I didn't reply. There was nothing to say.

16

Gordie and I reported as instructed on Monday morning, having filled in our forms. I'd said I was an experienced painter, which was sort of true, I'd painted Millie's house and done other odd bits of painting here and there. But I also looked upon the entire activity as something that anyone with half a brain could undertake pretty much successfully, something of a frivolous trade really, and I was more or less in agreement with Pazza's oft expressed opinion that if painters stopped paintin' altogether the world wouldn't actually come to an end, not in the way that it would if bricklayers like him stopped layin' bricks.

Gordie meanwhile was keen to do some basic labouring, the mindlessness of which more or less fitted in with his punk ethic. There was already a crew of three workers laying turf around and between the buildings in what seemed to me a forlorn effort to grow lawns in a place they just didn't belong, but who knows, with the further application of a lot of water and fertiliser and chemicals the grass might eventually take root. Regardless, the three blokes rolling out the turf seemed to be enjoying themselves no end. There was an older man, a New Zealander with long scraggly hair and a drooping moustache who looked like a burnt-out rock guitarist, together with two solid, blond-haired young men who spoke in sure-of-themselves educated Queensland accents and wore bandana-like scarves around their necks to soak up the sweat. They were medical students from Brisbane using their summer holidays to earn some cash, and they produced a pretty much constant sarcastic patter that the Kiwi chuckled and giggled along with. Gordie, also no slouch when it came to irony, was more than happy to join in.

I had to report to Al, who was acting as the head painter in lieu of Glen's reluctance to take on any kind of responsibility for anything. Al gave me a caulking gun with a tube of plastic goo and told me to fill in the gaps in the mortar in the transverse brick wall that bordered the steps up to the first floor of the library, prior to the wall being undercoated. So I set to work, filling in the holes. There were a lot of them; the wall had been hastily slapped up with the obvious intention that it would be painted. Pazza would not have approved, I was thinking; in regard to his own activities with the Department of Public Works in New South Wales, Pazza would often admit to having only laid six or seven bricks in a whole day, though he was very confident of the fact that those six or seven bricks had been laid very well. This was at a time when dickheads used to drive around with bumper stickers proclaiming things like Lay Chicks Not Bricks. Pazza didn't approve of that either. I was smiling to myself about all of this as I continued squeezing the gap filler into the gaps when I heard a snort behind me and turned around to see the site manager – hands on hips, sweat beading on his red face, a patchwork of stains on the blue singlet stretched over his seemingly-pregnant belly – standing there scrutinising my caulking. How the fuck had he been able to sneak up behind me so quietly, work boots and all? I nodded hello but he made no reply, just snorted again and walked off.

Five minutes later Al was behind me freaking out about the fact that Dennis – that was his name, the manager, Dennis – was freaking out about how much gap filler I was using. Don't blame me I said, blame the cunts that left all these gaps in the mortar. I know, said Al, trying as always to be conciliatory, but he says you're using too much filler and that it costs too much to just waste it like that. Maybe you should stuff the holes with paper and just fill in the top layer. Great, I said, that'll really give us a good solid finish. Look, that's the way it is, he said. All right, I said, so where do I get the paper? The school isn't open yet, there are no kids' schoolbooks for me to rip up and stick in there. Ok, ok, said Al, who often didn't have much of a sense of humour. I'll find you something. Just don't fill any more deep holes until I come back with some paper. Don't worry, I won't, I said, picking out the shallowest depression I could find and squeezing a bit of filler into it. Five minutes later Al was back with a sheet of black plastic left over from some concrete formwork. I put down the caulking gun and he handed me the cement-stained plastic and a Stanley knife to cut it up with. That should do he said, and walked off.

I cut up pieces of plastic and stuck them in the holes as instructed and then put the filler in on top and I was finished by morning tea. After morning tea I undercoated the wall, even though the filler was still damp. But it didn't matter. It would all dry out eventually. At lunchtime we ate sandwiches we'd made at the caravan the night before, and after lunch I started painting the window frames of a lightweight classroom building. It was a hot afternoon, Central Queensland in mid summer hot, hotter conditions than I'd ever tried to paint anything in before and it seemed as if the paint was actually drying on the brush before I'd even had a chance to apply it to the timber. I swirled a stick around the pot a few times but to no avail, the paint just seemed to be turning into mud. I slopped another thick brushfull onto the frame just in time to look up at the apoplectic face of Dennis who'd again managed to materialise beside me again without warning. 'Ow long you bin paintin' mate? he growled. I wasn't sure if it was actually a question he wanted answered or just a negative rhetorical observation, but I answered anyway: Coupla' years, I said. Yeah, well put some warter in yer paint, he grunted, before turning away and marching off. Sure enough, Al was around the corner a few minutes later brandishing a large plastic bottle of water and freaking out about what Dennis had told him about the thickness of my paint and how I needed to thin it down. Ok, ok, I said, even though to me this seemed as sacrilegious as putting ice cubes in beer.

Still, I watered down the paint and sure enough it flowed on a lot more easily. I wasn't certain of what the end result would be in terms of the quality of the coverage and how long it would last in the face of torrential downpours and baking sun, but that wasn't my problem was it? All I had to do was concentrate on not doing anything else to provoke the attention of Dennis, as two reprimands on my first day was obviously stretching the friendship. Plus, it was Al he was giving a hard time to, not me, so I felt a bit guilty about that as well. But I was also I annoyed with myself. It was such a simple thing, thinning the paint with water. Why hadn't I, who liked to think he was so clever, thought of it myself, and in fact I was a bit embarrassed, I looked like an idiot, and the only consolation I had was that Al was one of the few people I knew who wouldn't feel the need to use something like this against me at a later date because, while he may have been in possession of many weird and complex hang-ups, ego-driven insecurity wasn't one of them.

17

The rest of the working week passed without incident. I thinned the paint and painted as quickly and efficiently as I could and Dennis paid me no more personal visits. Nor did I notice him lurking anywhere nearby, though no doubt he had me under surveillance from a distance. But evidently I didn't fuck anything else up, because he not only left me in peace, he didn't badger Al about me again either. So I continued on the window frames and doors and eaves, the walls of the building that I was working on having already been coated by Glen and Lachlan.

It was a bit exhausting, starting at seven o'clock and continuing through to five or six in the Queensland summer heat, and I was generally too buggered to do anything much after knocking off except go back to the caravan, have a couple of beers and then flake out. Friday though we finished a bit earlier and went to the pub. Like many other people in town who wanted nothing other than to relax after a week of hard yakka, I took my beer outside to sit down on the front lawn for a while. It was a beautiful, soft evening, the fading sky clear, the air dry and warm, and I was hoping Maria would pull up in her Charger, as, having had no legitimate reason for visiting the hospital, I'd not seen her since the previous Friday night, most of which I couldn't actually remember.

The lawn was covered in small clusters of people smoking and drinking. I found a spot and sat down cross-legged and rested my beer on the grass and then lay on my back and looked up at the sky. It was the same as it always was: depthless, empty, devoid of any meaning other than the fact that it was there. I sat up again. A bloke sitting nearby was smiling at me. He had longish mousy hair and a thin droopy moustache and wore a blue and white striped shirt and jeans and cowboy boots. He looked a little over-dressed for Moranbah, even on a Friday night. It is big, yes. I must have looked puzzled, because he repeated his statement or question or whatever it was: it is big, yes. The sky, it is big. Oh, um, yes it is, I mumbled. It is, what do you say, gigantic, he continued, so much bigger than the sky where I come from. Where's that, I asked? Germany he answered. I had no idea what German skies were like, but I imagined them as mostly cloudy and sort of constipated. It's bigger than the sky where I come from too, I said, turning the topic back to something I knew about. And where is that, he asked? Sydney, I said. Yes, he said, nodding, I haff not been there. It is in the south, and I think everything in the south is smaller than it is here in the north, yes? Well, that's what they'll tell you in these parts, I replied. Ha-ha, he laughed, there is the same rivalry, north and south, in Germany too.

His name was Wolfgang, and there was a gentle mischievousness about him that was difficult not to like. So by way of keeping the conversation going, I asked him what was he doing in Central Queensland? He said he was an engineer, and that he was building mining machinery at one of the mines, Goonyella, which was about thirty kilometres north of town. Yes, he continued, I work for a German company. It is called Krupp. I nodded in recognition. Ah, you heard of us? Yes, indeed I had, the name had immediately conjured up the trenches of the Western Front, and of groups of sweating, grime-covered men in factories pouring giant flows of molten metal into big molds. I knew that Krupp had made Germany's cannons in the First World War, and made a fortune out of it as well, and that in the next war, Hitler's one, they'd used slave labourers from all over Europe to do the same thing.

Really, I said, I didn't know Krupp still existed, I thought all they did was make weapons in the wars. No, no, he said enthusiastically, no, no, now we make all kinds of big things, like radio telescopes to see far out into space and submarines that go really deep down in the deepest parts in the ocean, and mining machinery, really big pieces of machinery, yes, in Germany we just now made the biggest vehicle in the world.

Really, I replied, the biggest vehicle in the world? Yes, it is finished two years past. It is a bucket wheel excavator, just like we build here. It weighs 13 and a half thousand tonnes but it can still crawl on the ground under its own power. It is for mining lignite in the Ruhr area. You know what is lignite? Yes, I answered, it's brown coal. Yes, not like you have here, black coal. Anyway, until we built this machine, the crawler-transporter that carried the Apollo rocket from the factory in Florida to the launch pad was the biggest vehicle in the world, but now in Germany we build something bigger.

So will this machine you're building here be even bigger again, I asked? No, no, he chuckled, no it's not so big as in Germany. But still, it is big.

There was a pause in the conversation as I took a sip of beer and digested what he'd said. He offered me a cigarette and I thought why not and took it and then leant forward as he lit it for me with his lighter, not a plastic Bic like everybody else in town was carrying but an old metal one, the sort you had to fill with fluid. So why were they building the mining machine here, I asked? Why hadn't they just built it in Germany and shipped it out. He smiled again. Yes, I haff been a little bit confusing for you. I should say instead that we are only putting it together here. We build all the parts in Germany but it is too big to transport, there is no ship big enough to carry it, so we bring it out all in pieces and now we put it together at the site.

So, I asked, this excavator, is it like a dragline? I knew about draglines because I'd seen them in the *Four Corners* story on Moranbah. They were huge, and walked around on enormous feet, like something from *Star Wars*. Yes, he said, it is similar but where the dragline scoops the coal only with a single bucket, the excavator uses many buckets on a wheel. It is best for removing the top layers of coal. The dragline's limitation is that it can only dig below ground level. For example, it cannot dig into a cliff face, so it can be a little bit inefficient. This is why you need also the bucket wheel excavator.

He asked me what I was doing in Moranbah and I told him and he said oh yes and then stopped talking and took a drag of his cigarette and then a sip of his beer and we sat in silence for a moment. Then he started up the flow of information again. Do you know it was a German who first found coal here, in this place? No, I replied, I didn't know that. Yes, it was a German, an explorer, with the name Leichhardt. Do you know him? Yes, I did, you couldn't get through primary school without having the travails and triumphs of the early explorers rammed down your throat, it seemed to be the only history we had. Leichhardt though, like Burke and Wills, I remembered as being a bit mad, or hopeless, or maybe both. He'd tried to walk across the country from one side to the other and was never heard of again.

Ludwig Leichhardt, I said, I thought he disappeared somewhere out in the desert. Yes he did, Wolfgang answered, but before that he had made another travel, from the south of Queensland up to the north near Darwin, and on that trip he passed through this country here, and he saw the coal and made notice of it. Yes, there was nothing here then, just a wilderness and Aborigines hunting animals. Myself, I feel a little bit proud that it was a German who first discovered this place, and that now I am here helping to dig out this coal. Because there is such a lot of coal here, we will be mining this coal for another two or three hundred years, and this coal is so important to the world. Already it is going to Japan to industry to make cars and ships and airplanes and all the things needed to make the world a better place.

I nodded, I wasn't sure what to say about all this, but then I didn't have to say anything because Wolfgang was on a roll: It is really amazing, what technology can do. You have all this land, this wasteland, with nothing and nobody, and then machines come and they have the power to turn this wasteland into something that is useful to the world. Have you seen the mines? No, I admitted, I hadn't. But you must, he said, you must see them for yourself. The future is being dug out of the ground there before your eyes. Go out to Goonyella and look around and see the draglines working. And if I am there and not so busy, then I can show you some things. Really, you will not believe the power, the power of the machines.

18

My closest friend, Mark, or Spike as he was called by everyone, had not wanted to come with us, but rather, after the breakup of his relationship with his girlfriend Carol – Kevin's sister – had decided to go live by himself on the south coast. I'd sent word to him via my Mum of our address at the Coal Country Caravan Park and I got a surprise when I received a letter from him:

G'day mate
I'm living in a caravan too, in a park called the Shoalhaven Village in East Nowra. It's not too bad, full of dole bludgers and no-hopers. The bloke in the caravan next door, skinny as a rake, covered in tats and missing his front teeth knocked on my van's door the other day with a couple of beers and insisted I have one with him. We had a drink and he chain smoked a few rollies then stood up and stared at me and said, I'll tell you straight mate, you don't give me any shit and I won't give youse any. Ya got it! Then he picked up the rest of his six pack and left.

There's a single mother with a baby girl in the van on the other side. Her name's Nerida and she's pretty cute. I've said hello to her a couple of times but things haven't gone any further.

I really need a car down here. I have to get a bus into town to register for the dole and go to the shops and this van park is miles away from the surf. It's really hard for me to get there with my board. Maybe I'll try to hitch.

Anyway, I hope everything is going well up there in Queensland.

All the best,

Spike.

19

Sunday morning. Gordie, Kevin, Alka and I sitting outside the pub – waiting for it to open. We'd agreed to meet for a few games of pool with Gordie's new mates, the two medical students Alex and Hector along with the New Zealander Tim, as well as a mate of his, a fellow countryman who worked at the mines.

As the doors swung open at 11am it seemed as if a spell had been cast over the town by some playful demon: men, mostly on their own but some also in pairs or even groups appeared from various directions, somnambulating towards the siren's song emanating from the building. It reminded me of the scene in the film *The Time Machine* when Rod Taylor, having arrived in what seems like a paradise somewhere far in the distant future, is freaked out by the hitherto happy and contented young blond people he meets suddenly dropping whatever they're doing at the sound of a siren and marching off like automatons straight into the underground lair of the evil Morlocks, Neanderthal-types who are secretly farming the youthful Aryans for food. Actually, Rod Taylor had been flown in to Moranbah at some point in the 1970s to do a couple of sycophantic television advertisements promoting Utah's operations. On this particular Sunday, though, the square-jawed Hollywood Aussie was nowhere to be seen. Instead, a few minutes later Alex and Hector appeared as part of the impious morning procession, as did Tim and a thick-set bearded bloke in his thirties who introduced himself to us as Mack, or Mekk, as it sounded in his thick Kiwi accent. We all went into the pub.

Our plan was to have an informal pool tournament. With the eight of us making up four teams, each team could play the other three and then the two teams with the most wins would play off in a final. It was a bit early to start drinking but we did anyway, Alex and Hector being the most enthusiastic. And they could afford to be. Unlike inveterate manual workers such as Tim and Mack, who were staring down the barrel of a life of not much else but sweat, toil and liver problems, every day in Moranbah was a sort of holiday for the two medical students because the job itself was a holiday, getting paid to dig holes and shift dirt around being a novelty light years away from their usual responsibilities of training to be the caretakers of life and death. Which is also why Gordie, for whom every day was also a holiday because Johnny Rotten had said there was no future and that you may as well be pretty vacant, got on so well with them.

Our natural alliances determined the composition of the teams. Gordie and I fancied our chances as we'd both invested a lot of time on the pool tables of the pubs around the Rockdale area over the previous few years: the Arncliffe, the Banksia, the Grande, the St. George Tavern, Brighton Miller's, the Bexley North, even the Forest Inn, where Gordie and Pazza had been beaten up by bikies one night after being so reckless as to defeat them on the green baize. But, Gordie and I weren't alone in fancying ourselves, playing pool was something a lot of young men were good at, or at least liked to think they were, even bourgeois medical students. Alka was no slouch either, he might have been crazy but he had a great eye for detail. And Kevin could hold up his end too, which was why I found it puzzling that, as the game between him and Alka on the one side and the junior doctors on the other wore on, the two Kiwis began to dissolve into fits of giggles every time he lined up a shot. The explanation became clear though after Kevin sunk a ball and Tim managed to stop laughing long enough to congratulate him – noish one eh, Bluetongue – before falling about again in fits of laughter. Kevin gave him a dirty though also puzzled look, and moved to set up his next shot. As his shooting arm drew the cue backwards I suddenly saw the source of all the mirth: as his beady eyes narrowed in concentration Kevin's tongue came slithering and curling out of the left side of his mouth, transforming him for anyone with a malicious sense of humour – and really, who in this ersatz outback shithole didn't possess some sort of nasty streak – into the image of a fat lizard trying to catch a fly.

Go Bluetongue. Kevin potted the next ball as well, as Gordie also picked up on the joke and joined in the laughter, thereby displaying one of his most annoying traits, the propensity to sell out his taken-for-granted friends in order to suck up to total strangers who he thought it might be either cool or useful to establish relations with. Lachlan was a master of the same maneuver, often making fun of one of us in front of someone, usually a woman, who he was trying to impress, and it never failed to annoy me. In Gordie's case, I was thinking, as I watched Kevin line up his next ball, it doubly annoyed me because earlier in the week he'd criticised me for agreeing with people too much. You're an agreer, he'd said, after a conversation we'd had with Carl, a jazz drummer from Brisbane who was working as a labourer on the fitting out of the classrooms and who I thought was quite a nice bloke with some interesting things to say; but no, for Gordie all the conversation had demonstrated was that I was an agreer, a verb turned noun I wasn't sure even actually existed but which, the tone in Gordie's voice indicated, was a weak and pathetic and decidedly un-Punk thing to be. But making fun of your friends in order to ingratiate yourself with strangers was ok, apparently. Fuck youse, said Kevin, his right arm starting to shake as the heckling finally got to him and he messed up his shot, the cue ball dribbling across the table and into the opposite pocket.

And so on it went, the Kiwis, several pots later, easily accounting for Gordie and myself in the playoff. We shook hands and agreed on how much fun it had been and I suggested we should do it again next Sunday. No, not next Sunday, said Tim. I'm going to put down a Hangi, and you're all invited. It'll be grate: we can hev a few beers and watch the cruckit. Yis, it'ull be grate, eh. Sure we said, that'll be great. We'll be there.

What's a Hangi? I asked as we stumbled across town to the golf club where we'd agreed to meet Al and Lachlan for lunch. Fucked if I know, said Gordie.

20

In order to get into the golf club you needed a collared shirt and shoes. Alka had loaned Gordie a pink polo shirt and a pair of smart white casual loafers, neither of which fitted him properly in any sense, but still they got us through the door. Al and Lachlan were already at a table in the dining room, sipping beers and looking out at small groups of checked pants-wearing Utah managers and their lackeys dragging overloaded golf bags up and down the stunted, brownish fairways in the hot sun of the early afternoon. Look at these cunts, they're mad, said Lachlan. We agreed, much better a cool beer and roast beef, potatoes and gravy in the air-conditioned comfort of the club.

We went over and took our plastic trays from the pile and joined the queue at the bain marie, where a chubby woman on the edge of middle age, red-faced from the constant heat of the kitchen, loaded up our plates with the traditional Sunday fare, which to me was also something of a novelty as in my family we'd always eaten the weekend roast on Saturday night. I took Gordie's plate back to the table for him while he went to the bar to get us a drink. On the other side of the big window grown men continued to encourage little white balls to fall into holes in the ground. I'd read somewhere that after the Bolshevik Revolution golf had been banned in the Soviet Union. This seemed sensible to me. The game summed up almost everything that was wrong with the world: weasel-like cap-doffers doing all the fetching and toting for fat bastards with bad dress sense and pockets full of cash, while other flunkies coaxed all that European-style grass along with sprinklers and fertiliser in a place where in reality scrubby bush was the only thing that would actually thrive. Maybe we should have a game of golf, Al said. We looked at him and laughed.

But Al took the ethics of small business capitalism seriously, and so he was serious enough about having a round of golf too, pointing out that it was only a nine-hole course. Lachlan told him that it was too hot, short course or not. I didn't bother to voice my ideological objections: this would have only encouraged Gordie to say that a game was a good idea just to spite me. Actually, truth be told I was no stranger to golf myself, I'd played off and on throughout high school, I just found it boring, apart that is from the burst of focused concentration when you were on the putting green, a brief patch of enjoyment which always took far too much effort to get to. Of course, if I'd had someone to carry my clubs around for me I might have felt differently about it. Anyway, the entrepreneur in Al had moved on. It bothered him that Kevin and Alka didn't have anything to do he said, that they earned no money, that they hung around the caravan all day sleeping and drinking cups of tea and reading magazines and science fiction books they'd gotten from the library. So he suggested that after lunch we take them down to the school and get them to help us finish the interior of the class-room we'd been working on. It was Sunday, Dennis wouldn't be around to hassle us, they could give us a hand and we could give them a bit of cash for it. Lachlan and I agreed: it seemed like a good idea. Count me out, said Gordie. Sunday's my day of rest. I'm goin' back to the pub.

We finished lunch and went back to the caravan. They both liked the idea: Kevin was bored and, in his quiet way, he was desperate for something constructive to do, while Alka, whose medication probably made him impervious to boredom, was still excited at the prospect of something different. I on the other hand could feel a headache coming on, the sort I always got from drinking at lunchtime, let alone before lunch, so I took some codeine. We all had a cup of tea and then drove over to the school, minus Gordie, who'd gone back to the pub, and Glen, who had gone to join him. Al set Kevin and Alka up with brushes and paint and gave them the storeroom to take care of. It was a small windowless room attached to the main class-room and Al wanted them to undercoat it, a simple enough task. I went back to the window frames I'd been working on when we'd knocked off on

Friday afternoon while Lachlan and Al continued with the walls, Lachlan doing the rolling with Al following him and doing the cutting in. We were getting to be quite a good team.

Al went to check on Kevin and Alka now and then to make sure it was all going ok, emerging from the storeroom with an impish grin on his face each time. Moving along to paint the window closest to the storeroom, I could hear what sounded like nothing so much as two boxers slugging it out in the ring, so I put down my paint pot and brush and poked my own head around the doorframe to have a look. Kevin, tongue poking furiously out of the corner of his mouth, was up on a ladder attacking the ceiling while Alka was coating the walls, the slap and splatter of their brushes as they flung them with reckless enthusiasm against the hard plasterboard surfaces making it sound for all the world as if they were in there punching each other. We'd covered the floor with drop sheets before they started and they'd both stripped down to their underpants because it was hot and humid in the little box of a room. This was fortunate, because they seemed to have gotten almost as much paint on themselves as on the walls and the ceiling.

I laughed, and went back to my window frame. It was starting to get dark, we'd been at it now for a few hours and I was thinking that I'd suggest to Al that we should probably finish up soon when Kevin, white paint splattered all over his face and pudgy, sweating torso, emerged from the room. Mate, he said to me, I've got the shits. What's wrong Kev, I asked, what have you got the shits about? No mate, he insisted, no, I mean I've got the shits, like, you know, diarrhea. It must have been the pie I got from the shop for lunch. I need to get to a toilet. Hmm, I thought. The toilet in the building we were working in wasn't connected yet, and the buildings that were hooked up to the sewer were locked and Dennis had the keys. So I pulled out my car keys and handed them to him, as well as giving him my cleaning-up cloth so he could wipe the wet paint off himself before he got into the car. As he scurried out the door I went back to the window, but I'd only had time to load up my brush when the unmistakable metallic crunch of one automobile making contact with another made me drop the brush back into the pot. What the fuck, said Al, and we darted outside just in time to see Kevin – who'd backed the rear of my Ford into the front of Al's Holden – fishtailing away in a spray of gravel.

We went over to the Holden and inspected the damage in the shadowy light from the classroom windows: it didn't look too bad, just a bit of buckling of the bumper bar. I hoped the injury to my vehicle would be as minimal. That was quite a feat, said Lachlan: there are only two cars in a three-kilometre radius of here and he's managed to smash one of 'em into the other one.

Poor Bluetongue, it just hadn't been his day.

21

We didn't need to wait until the following Sunday to find out what a Hangi was. Tim was so excited that he'd spent all week talking it up as he rolled out the turf. It sounded like a barbeque mixed with a roast dinner: you dug a hole, lined the bottom of the hole with rocks, then made a fire on top of the rocks and tended it for a while until the rocks were very hot, then you wrapped a piece of meat in foil, lay it on the hot rocks and covered everything over with some of the dirt you'd dug out. After a few hours you dug it all up again, by which point the meat was 'tinder ezz'. Apparently, Maoris had invented it. Tim had been in negotiations for some time with the town butcher, who had undertaken to supply him with the carcass of a small pig. Of course, Tim would have preferred to have gone out and shot a wild pig for himself, but unfortunately he didn't have a gun. Nor it seemed did anyone else he knew in town, or at least, not one that they were prepared to lend him.

The week passed, our days spent working on the school, our nights drinking and playing pool at the pub. Sunday was warm and overcast, but it didn't look like rain. We went our separate ways in the morning and met up back at the caravan at lunchtime and then, armed with the ubiquitous carton of XXXX, made our way down to Tim's van at the other end of the park. It was the last in the row and there was a patch of mangy grass between the annex and the fence. This was where he'd dug the cooking pit. He'd set up some deck chairs next to the annex and was sitting in one of them drinking a beer, next to Mack and a woman with curly black hair. Aw, yiss, he said, standing up to greet us, gud to see yuz all. Come and hev a sut down und a beer und a chun wag. So that's the Hangi is it, Gordie said, pointing at the pile of newly churned dirt? Yiss, it's grate usn't ut, answered Mack enthusiastically. Yiss, added the woman, and there's a lovely little pug in there, isn't there Tum. You betcha he answered, his gaze briefly traversing all of us. This is moi wife he gestured, nodding towards the woman, Olga, Olga from the Volga, ha ha. I hope yuz all brought ya appetites with yuz. Yeah mate, no worries on that score, Lachlan answered, giving Tess, who was next to him, a pat on her flank. She replied with a yawn and went to lie down next to the fire pit. Fuck eh, what a horse, chuckled Mack, who hadn't encountered her before.

Are you Russian, I asked Olga? No, she laughed, don't lusten to hum she said, nodding towards Tim, he's a duckhid. I felt a bit silly, as she was obviously no more Russian than I was, but I hadn't been able to think of anything else to say to her.

Suddenly I heard the distinctive throb of Maria's Charger pulling up behind the caravan. I looked up as Tim said, oh yiss, I invited a couple of girls I met at the club the other day as well. Despite having been thinking about Maria pretty much constantly over the last little while, I was still surprised by how good it was to see her as she came around the corner of the caravan wearing a bright green shift dress and sandals and carrying a bottle of Jack Daniels, followed by Karen who, in stone-washed jeans and a blue and white striped tank top, was clutching two large bottles of coke. They said hello to Tim who then introduced them to Olga and Mack, Olga standing up and saying that she'd go into the kitchen and get them some glasses. Thanks said Maria, turning to us and announcing hello, I'm Maria. And I'm Karen, added her friend. It was clear from the absence of any kind of familiarity on Maria's part that she had retained absolutely nothing of our night on the barbs. Fuck, I thought, I'll have to start all over again. She glanced at Tess and then looked back at me and said, oh yeah, I remember seeing you with your dog the other day.

She's my dog, not his, Lachlan immediately chipped in.

Oh really said Maria and smiled at him. We all smiled and introduced ourselves, keeping silent about our previous encounter; one of the great things about drugs was how deceitful they made you: it would have been very poor form to bring up the subject of barbiturates in front of Tim, Olga and Mack, people we didn't know very well.

Maria looked us over. I've seen you boys around she said, so what do you do here, she asked? Gordie laughed.

We're working on the new primary school they're building, I answered. We're painters. And labourers added Gordie.

Painting, that must be fun she replied.

Yeah sometimes it can be I answered, smiling to myself at the thought of Kevin and Alka on the job the previous Sunday.

What about you girls I asked?

We're nurses said Karen, we work at the hospital.

Actually we're midwives added Maria.

Really I said, well luckily we've had no reason to visit the hospital yet, nor have we needed a midwife.

Everyone laughed at this and I sat back, quite pleased with my efforts at banter.

Olga returned from the caravan with some plastic cups and Gordie asked if we could put our beers in their fridge. Tim said he had plenty of cold stubbies and got up and went into the caravan, returning with a beer for each of us and a fresh one for Mack, along with a bottle opener to knock the tops off. He'd set up a portable television on a stool with a connecting extension cord running into the caravan. Australia and New Zealand were playing a one-day cricket match. Now that we'd all settled in with a drink, Tim turned his attention to the cricket. Aw choice, he exclaimed as the Kiwi batsman Bruce Edgar hit a boundary. The rest of us chatted away about Moranbah and what we thought of it for a while until Tim went over to the TV and turned up the volume. It was the last ball of the match and the Kiwis needed to hit a six to tie the result. The way they'd been playing it wasn't impossible and I could hear the commentator Bill Lawry saying that it looked as if the Australians had told the umpires that they were going to bowl this last ball underarm. This was so that there was no chance of it being hit for a six. Fuck thet said Mack. I could hardly believe my eyes as

Trevor Chappell then stepped up to the crease and rolled the ball along the surface of the wicket. The batsman, Brian McKechnie, tapped it forward when it reached him and then threw his bat away in disgust, proceeding to walk off. Aw fuck no said Tim angrily and then added what a duckhid. No one else said anything for a moment until eventually Olga observed: Underarm, that's jist trejuck eh.

Frowning, Tim took a long swig of his beer and then glared at us all. You fucking Aussie cheats he said. Steady on mate said Lachlan, it's not our fault. Tim put his beer down and stared at him. Git out the lot of yuz he shouted. I mean it, fuck off now before I git really angry. What about us asked Maria plaintively? Aw, youse girls can stay he answered as he shook his head and got up and went into the caravan, emerging with our carton of XXXX which he carried over to Gordie to emphasise how serious he was about us leaving. Gordie laughed in an embarrassed kind of way but Lachlan had already gotten up and walked away. The rest of us followed. What should we do now Kevin asked as we passed the Charger? Go and drink our fucken carton Lachlan answered. Fuck this, said Gordie, I was really looking forward to some of that pork. Meanwhile I pondered the fact that I'd need another opportunity to get to know Maria.

22

We sat in our hot annex drinking the slowly warming stubbies and discussing the underarm incident. Richie Benaud had said it was a disgraceful performance by Australia. Carl the drummer, who lived in a caravan nearby, had joined us. He was something of a cricket expert and assured us that there was nothing in the rules that prevented such an action, even though it was hardly in what they called the 'spirit of the game'. Fuck 'em said Gordie, I'm glad we beat the cunts. Me too I added, though it's a shame about the Hangi. This seemed to be the general consensus.

Well, said Al, maybe he'll calm down and invite us to another one.

Not on your Nellie said Lachlan, we're lucky we got out of there alive.

Everyone laughed.

We finished the beers and went to the pizza shop and then had an early night.

The next day after work Gordie reported that Tim had indeed calmed down and had said that there were no hard feelings and that we should put it all in the past. However, no more social invitations had been forthcoming.

So we continued to wake up hungover in the pale early light and make tea and toast in the humid little caravan kitchen before heading over to the school to sweat it out under the relentless Queensland sun. The hot days were hard going for the landscapers and Gordie was unyielding in his protestations as to how easy we painters had it (working indoors half the time!) compared to the hard yakka he and his comrades put in for more or less the same money. I had an idea to placate him by way of Jesus' parable of the complaining vineyard workers, but thought better of it.

With the application of plenty of water the paint was flowing on well and we were beginning to take a certain pride in our work. The buildings were looking good inside and out and I would have liked to be staying until the job was finished to see how it all came together, but Dennis had only signed me on for four weeks. So I turned up, did my job and then repaired to the pub or to the caravan. Kevin and Alka meanwhile had discovered the town library and put in much of their time there watching videos, as our caravan had no television, only a radio. Tess spent her time dozing in the annex waiting for Lachlan to come home and dish her out a giant tin of dogfood. It was hot and monotonous. If this was life in the working class I realised why I had been avoiding it for so long.

I was opening a tin of paint with a screwdriver one day just after morning tea when it jumped off the rim and skidded across the lid and impaled the forefinger of my left hand, with which I was steadying the can. The screwdriver was stuck in the side of my finger just above the joint and when I pulled it out the pain was so intense I thought I was going to faint. Blood spurted out and into my paint tray mixing with the government-issue cream paint that the tray already held. I pulled out my hankie, I tried never to go anywhere without a hankie (monogrammed with an L which Millie used to give me for birthdays) and wrapped it around the wound. Aside from the pain my finger wouldn't move, I couldn't bend it at the joint. I went over to the building Al was working on and showed him. We agreed I needed to go to the hospital and Al said he'd take me and ran over to the office to tell Dennis. I showed my finger to Lachlan and Glen. Far out was Glen's comment. Jeez mate Lachlan said that doesn't look too good. Al came back and I asked him what Dennis had said. He laughed and said he'd said Don't be too long. Dickhead. We went out and climbed into Al's panel van.

Al had always been a careful, thoughtful driver and despite the fact that my white handkerchief bandage was quickly reaching its blood saturation limits he took it slowly through Moranbah's ersatz suburban streets until we saw the big EMERGENCY sign in white letters on a red background with an arrow pointing to the left. Moranbah hospital was a one-storey brick building set behind a big car park. Al parked and we got out and walked over to the Emergency department where an ambulance was backed up to the entrance. We went inside and stopped at the desk where a nurse was sitting looking through some files. I looked across the room to an alcove where a man lay on a bed while a man who (from his white coat and the stethoscope around his neck) was obviously a doctor and two nurses busied themselves around him. One of them was Maria, her dark hair piled up on her head.

Yes and what can we do for you? asked the desk nurse as she looked us up and down. I've stabbed myself I said holding up my hand. Not intentional was it she said more as a statement than a question. Been here before? No I said. What's your name, date of birth and address? Once she had the paperwork done she told Al to take a seat in the waiting room and took my hand and unwrapped the hankie from my finger from which blood was still issuing. Oh that looks nasty she said and wrapped the hankie back on it and led me over to another alcove bed and told me to lie down. Then she came back with some antiseptic, washed my finger down and then wrapped a piece of gauze around it. The doctor will see you as soon as he's free she said and then walked off.

Immersed in the pungent smell of the hospital, a mixture of disinfectant, bottled oxygen and plastic, I lay on the bed wondering what had happened to the patient in the other bed; maybe he'd had a stroke or a heart attack or been injured in a mining accident. Whatever it was it seemed to be under control as the doctor had drifted over to the front desk and was talking to the nurse there.

Maria had noticed me and came over to my bed. So, she smiled, here you are and you didn't even need to get pregnant to do it. No, I said, so why aren't you delivering babies? I'm only a part-time midwife she answered, obstetrics isn't busy enough to keep us dedicated full time. Anyway, what happened to you? I told her. Careless boy she said, unwrapping the makeshift dressing. I reckon it will be ok, I don't think your arm will have to come off, but we'll see what the doctor says. Thanks I said smiling, and asked what happened to him?, nodding in the direction of the other patient. I can't tell you she said with a serious look on her face.

The doctor, a youngish Indian man, came and stood by the bed. Hello he said, I'm Doctor Laxman. What has happened to you? I told him and held out my hand. He took it, unwrapped the makeshift bandage and looked at my finger and asked me to move it up and down. I said I couldn't. Hmm he sighed perhaps you have damaged the tendon. We need to look at it with the ultrasound. He turned to Maria: Nurse could you get the ultrasound machine please. She went across to the other side of the room and returned with a small trolley with what I assumed was the ultrasound machine perched on top. I'd heard of ultrasound but had never had one before. Maria washed my finger with more disinfectant, then the doctor placed my hand flat on the movable bedside table they use to give you meals, with my injured finger pointing straight out.

He squirted some goo out of a plastic tube onto the top of my finger and then turned the machine on and picked up what looked like a small hammer with a connecting cable and gently ran the smooth metal head along my wounded finger. There was a strange whooshing sound that came and went. Ok he said, looking at a video screen, there is the tendon and it looks intact, though a little swollen. Perhaps you've bruised it, which would account for the lack of movement. What's that noise I asked? It's your blood pulsing he answered, so, good to know your heart is still doing its job, yes? He chuckled. I think your finger will be ok if you rest it for a few days. I'll sew up the wound and put a small splint on to keep your finger still, then you can go. I asked Maria to go out to the waiting room and tell Al what was happening. Half an hour later we were back in the car park, with instructions for me to come back in a week to check for infection and get the stiches out.

23

I decided to take the next day off work. The injury was to my left hand so I could still paint with my right, but it would be a good idea to take it easy as the doctor had said. This meant I got to sleep in, but the others made so much noise getting up and having their breakfast that it didn't really matter. Lachlan brought me a mug of tea, which was nice. After they left I went over to the shower block and had a shower, something I didn't normally have time for in the morning. I made sure to keep my left hand away from the water and anyway it was only a quick shower as the damp brick building was full of mosquitos.

I went back to the caravan unsure of what to do with myself. Kevin and Alka were heading off to the library so I decided to go with them. Good said Kevin we can take your car. I said ok as long as he drove.

Kevin pulled up outside the library and we got out of the car and headed in. It was a low-slung building that looked like it would have been nominated for an architecture award or two. We went through the front doors into the welcome cool of the air-conditioned interior. Kevin and Alka were proposing to watch *Star Wars*, but since I'd already seen it I don't know how many times (as had they) I decided to peruse the bookshelves in search of the gardening and landscaping section. I had a vague idea of the call number, it was in the 700s, and soon found it. I found a couple of books that fitted what I was looking for. For the previous year or so I'd been mowing people's lawns. I suppose you would have called it a small business: I advertised in the local paper and people rang me up and asked me to mow their lawn. My most common type of customer was an ageing woman living on her own after her husband had died. All alone in their suburban castles these women were finding it difficult to manage the home maintenance tasks which their men had been responsible for before getting cancer or having a heart attack or whatever. I found these women with their large, empty homes incredibly sad. In addition to mowing the lawn, and after the inevitable cup of tea they made me, they would often ask me if I could do garden and yard work for them, such as removing old gardens, putting new gardens in and so forth; so without any training and no real idea of what I was doing I would have a go at these small scale landscaping jobs. So now I was thinking that perhaps I should read up on the area and try to pick up some skills and ideas. There were a few suitable books on the shelf so I picked out *Practical Home Landscaping* and *Landscaping Projects: A Complete Guide* and went up to the loans desk, joined the library, then checked out the two books.

I found Kevin and Alka in a video viewing room watching Obi-Wan Kenobi revealing his true identity to Luke Skywalker. I told them I was leaving and that they could bring the car back later. Then I walked back to the caravan carrying the books, new library card in my pocket. The sun was bright and hot and the air was muggy. I needed, I thought as I walked the footpath-less suburban streets, to get a hat. Sweat pouring down my fore-head and over my eyebrows and sunglasses, I passed through the front gate of the Coal Country Caravan Park and through the jumble of vans to the one that we occupied. Tess raised her head and looked at me as I pushed open the annex door flap. I made a cup of tea and took it back into the annex and sat down at the table and leafed through the books. My grand-mother always used to say that the best thing to cool you down on a hot day was a hot cup of tea. I never understood the logic but she seemed to be right, I thought, as I sat inside the canvas walls and sipped at the mug full of hot brown liquid.

The books contained plenty of good illustrations and useful informa-tion for a novice like me. The last so-called landscaping job I'd done was in Sylvania Waters, a suburban development on a former mangrove ecosystem in the Sutherland Shire in southern Sydney that would become famous as the home of the obstreperous Noeline in Australia's first reality TV show.

In the 1960s developers had invaded the area, one of many mangrove land-scapes that formed the border between land and sea around the edges of Botany Bay, turning the web of mangrove trees and marine habitats into a network of concreted canals, suburban streets and brick houses. The idea was that as well as parking your car out the front of your house you could tie your boat up out the back. It was in a backyard on one of these canals behind a single-storey brick veneer home that I had undertaken some work for yet another widowed woman.

In the middle of this particular backyard, which was a flat surface of lawn butting up against a canal, were two kidney-shaped gardens, edged by low cement borders and filled with wilting and dying plants. The owner had no interest in gardening she said, it had been her husband's thing and we agreed that I should pull the plants out, smooth out the soil and put down black plastic sheeting and cover this with a layer of white river stones. So I ordered a tonne of river stones from the landscaping supplier in Kogarah. Kevin owned an old purple Valiant utility, quite a rare beast, there were few Valiant utes around, much more common were the sedans favoured by Mediterranean families, who probably wouldn't have objected to the purple colour scheme but would have had no use for a ute. Kevin had bought it cheap from his brother-in-law, a bass player in a Led Zeppelin covers band, and he was more than happy to loan it to me. So I went around to his place to pick it up. It was almost twenty years old and drifted all over the road, the steering linkages needed replacing. But with concentration I got it to the landscaping supplier in one piece and parked it their yard. After I'd been into the office and paid I stood with the manager and watched as a front-end loader scooped up a load of white stones from a big pile and trundled over to the ridiculous-looking beast and positioned the bucket over the carry-ing tray. The driver tipped the bucket up and a slurry of stones cascaded into the back of the vehicle. As the tray filled, the back half of the Valiant began to sink towards the ground like a collapsing soufflé. It wasn't just the steering that was crook, the springs were obviously no good either. I held my breath as the rear bumper got closer and closer to the ground. Luckily the rain of stones ended before the back of the ute's body hit the earth or the rear wheels were obscured by the sunken rear mudguards. The manager turned and grinned at me, Just made it he said with a laugh.

I backed out of the yard with the heavy load bouncing up and down on the uneven surface. But once I got onto the highway and headed towards Sylvania Waters the weight seemed to have a positive effect and the Valiant became a little easier to steer, though each time I passed over a bump in the road the back end went up and down like a seesaw and an excruciating scraping sound issued from under the vehicle. But I made it to Sylvania Waters, and pulled into the driveway and climbed out, shaking from the stress and regretting that I'd stopped smoking, as a calming cigarette would have been just the ticket to settle my nerves. I'd left my wheelbarrow and shovel in the backyard on a previous visit so I went around the back to get them as a police helicopter flying up the canal swooped down and flew around in a circle above me. Apparently satisfied that I was working legitimately rather than about to perform a break and enter, it flew off along the canal and I gathered up the barrow and began shifting the stones.

Why hadn't I got them delivered to the site I wondered, as I finished my tea in the annex? Then I wouldn't have had the stress of dealing with Kevin's old Valiant and the stones would have been in a pile in the driveway and shifting them from there would have been a lot easier than having to shovel them out of the back of the ute first. Because it was cheaper to pick them up rather than pay the delivery fee, that's why. I needed to become much more professional, I thought, as I studied a garden plan in *Practical Home Landscaping*.

24

I went to work the next day. I didn't want to lose another day's pay. I'd been to the pharmacy in the town square the previous afternoon and bought a lightweight arm sling, which would keep my finger out of harm's way, and I would be doing all my painting with my right hand. Al said he would help me with the tins of paint and any other two-handed tasks.

Besides the money, I really enjoyed the work. Painting might have been a bit of a mindless activity, but it gave you a real sense of satisfaction and achievement as you turned the original raw material, be it metal, plastic, wood, gyprock, whatever, into a neat, finished product. I suppose it appealed to my obsession with creating order from chaos, something I'd lived with since childhood. When I was younger I loved making model planes, tanks and cars for the same reason; getting all the small pieces and fusing them into a coherent and fixed whole. I'm sure that painting was like this for Lachlan too, and it was obvious that it was for Al. We were all a bit obsessive. As for Glen, who knows, but as he seemed in a permanent zone of chaos it was hard to say whether or not the paint helped. Pazza was right, the world wouldn't come to an end if painters stopped painting, but if they did, it certainly wouldn't look as beautiful.

So I continued to coat the windows and doors. The school was looking good. Lachlan, Al and Glen had finished the exterior walls of the buildings, and all were now a uniform shade of pale cream, which seemed well suited to the sun-soaked environment. Grass, laid by Gordie, Alex, Hector and Tim, while not exactly thriving in the heat, covered most of the school grounds, and an asphalt assembly and sports area sat in the centre of the clutch of buildings. This made me think of my primary school, which had been similarly asphalted. In the centre of this formal space a large yellow circle had been painted on the ground. If you had been disobedient you were forced to sit inside this circle at lunchtime: sort of a circular version of the naughty corner. This punishment was known as 'the circle' and it was meted out only to boys, not girls. So on a baking hot summer day you would find yourself sitting on the playground surface without a hat, with the bare skin of your legs on the hot asphalt as sweat poured down your face. It reminded me of a film which was often on TV at the time called *The Hill*, in which a sadistic sergeant played by Harry Andrews forced Sean Connery, carrying a heavy backpack, to incessantly run up and down a sand hill in a British Army prison in the North African desert.

As I got to the bottom of my tin of paint I wondered to what tortures the children soon to take up their education here would be condemned, though maybe being forced to grow up in this so-called town stuck out in the middle of nowhere, while dad worked at the mine and mum stayed home and was bored to death, would be punishment enough. Anyway, I should get on with the job; I needed more paint so I needed to find Al. He was in the library with Glen and Lachlan, so I loped up the short flight of stairs next to the wall I'd filled and painted on my first day. They were in the main library room, sitting in a cloud of smoke in a circle on the floor with a mixing bowl in front of them from which Lachlan was packing Al's favourite bamboo bong. It's alright for some I said, walking up and sitting down. Good timing said Lachlan, before putting the neck of the bong to his lips and flicking a Bic lighter over the cone. He pulled on it hard as the flame was sucked downwards and water bubbled and the mix glowed in the cone. Bong pulling was something of a championship sport for Lachlan and he stopped pulling for a moment, drew some breath and then continued until the cone was empty. Then he gave a convulsive cough as he released a lungful of smoke.

Lachlan had grown up in a small Victorian terrace house in Rockdale with his three brothers and sister and their Mum and Dad. At her funeral in the 1990s, John, the eldest sibling, had described their mother Eileen – usually shorted to just Eil – as a true Christian in every sense. A big woman with an earthy presence, she was a committed Catholic, possessed of an enormous generosity of spirit; to the extent that all were welcome in the family home, which became something of a drop-in centre for the many mates of the three brothers. On weekend days it was not unusual to find groups of young men sitting on the small sofas in the tiny lounge room, or sitting around the table in the kitchen drinking cups of tea, while the only girl in the house stayed in her room reading, doing her schoolwork and keeping out of sight of the raucous young blokes. Lachlan's father meanwhile, as short and skinny as his wife was tall and solid, spent his time relaxing in his shorty pyjamas on his bed in the front bedroom, drinking cans of KB lager and listening to the horse races on the radio, having placed bets with a woman a few doors down the street (a distant relative of my mother), who was an SP bookmaker. He would occasionally venture out, passing through the lounge room on his way to the toilet and uttering his trademark hello of *Owyagoin boys* to the crowd of itinerant young men who appeared to have taken over his house. Completing the family were two small fox terriers: a black and white one called Jimmy, and a brown and white called Brown, perhaps because it was just the obvious choice. Jimmy was epileptic, had a staggering gait and a tendency to fall asleep on the lounge after one of his fits and then wake up and bite the person sitting next to him. Brown on the other hand no had major ailments but was of a surly disposition, and only ever responded to Eil and her call of *Brow-when*, which stretched the name out into a form of an elongated, drawling statement, the aural partner to the pervasive smell of dog that permeated the room. The house was located in a street a short distance from the end of one of the airport runways, and landing and departing airliners screamed overhead at all hours, shaking the windows, rattling the beer cans and drowning out conversation with a sickening, deafening roar.

Lachlan passed the bong and the lighter to me and I packed a small-ish cone, as my lungs weren't as strong as his and the mix was heavy with tobacco. Shouldn't we be keeping an eye out for Dennis? I asked before I lit it up. That fat fuck is too lazy to climb up the stairs Glen mumbled and we all laughed. I finished, exhaled the smoke and passed on to Glen. Where did you get this stuff? I asked. A bloke at the pub answered Al.

I was surprised Al was ok with sitting down on the job like this, as he liked to run a tight ship. But then, drugs were something he always treated with a degree of ritualistic respect. He took his turn and we continued until the mix was finished. Marijuana in the morning always gave me a headache, but it was, no pun intended, actually smoko time, and so Lachlan got up and went and got the mugs, thermos and tea bags and we made morning tea, the guzzling of which helped to soothe my throbbing head. Half an hour later I was back downstairs with a full tin of paint, working on the windows, singing Velvet Underground songs to myself and wishing we'd had some biscuits to go with the tea.

25

The month I had signed on for ended the following Friday, so I finished up. Al, Lachlan and Glen would stay on for another couple of weeks to finish the job. The landscaping was completed, so Gordie finished work as well.

Boredom loomed, so on the weekend I suggested that on the Monday morning we go out to one of the coalmines for a look. Kevin and Alka wanted to come too, as they had nothing else to do.

After the painters had headed off to work and we'd had another mug of tea we got into my Ford and headed north out of town, past the drive-in, which was showing *The Blue Lagoon* and *Breaker Morant* (a perverse double), neither of which we'd been to see. We continued out into the Central Queensland bush: undulating, mostly flat land, covered in grasses, wattle and sparsely situated gum trees. Goonyella mine was about 30 kilometres north of town straight up the only road in that direction. It was an open cut mine and so covered a huge area, too big to fence, so there was no entrance gate, just a big sign by the side of the road a couple of kilometres out.

Closer to the site were some temporary buildings: an administration block and a canteen. Everything was temporary and contingent around here, that was the nature of ripping resources out of the land; it was an impermanent and provisional activity from which the participants intended to bugger off as soon as the money ran out. I parked the car in the parking area and we got out. It was a sunny day again, the sky bright blue while the earth all around us, which should have been a shade of ochre, was a greyish black, covered in coal dust. We crossed the black earth to the canteen and Kevin pushed open the door and we went into the air-conditioned interior. Bearded, burly men in navy blue overalls sat around tables tucking into plates of bacon and eggs. Their conversations paused as we entered and they looked at us

with suspicion. Who the fuck were we? Having always been a trade union-
ist I naively felt a sense of solidarity with them, as I knew the history of
the miner's union. But the atmosphere wasn't inviting much comradeship.
Bewdy, I'm gettin' some bacon and eggs said Gordie, and we all went up
to the counter and ordered bacon and eggs, tea and toast. This was good;
none of us had had a proper breakfast for weeks.

These blokes look like they work hard said Alka.

Bullshit answered Gordie, machines do it all for 'em.

Yeah but, I said, determined to argue with him, they put in long hours
looking after the machines. Look they're having their breakfast now after
working all night.

Yeah well whatever.

Once I finished my bacon and eggs I got up and went over to the admin
building to see if Wolfgang was around. I asked for him at the desk and the
desk woman went and got him. I explained that I'd brought the boys along
with me, he'd met them at the pub by this point, and he said sure, he'd take
us over and show us the mine. I went back to the canteen to collect the
three while Wolfgang went to pick up a minibus. They'd finished eating so
we went and stood outside. Wolfgang pulled up in the Toyota bus, painted
white with a red stripe along the side, like all the mine vehicles, and coated
with a layer of black dust.

We climbed in and sat down and Wolfgang headed in the direction of
the mine pit. He pulled up beside a viewing platform and said Ok my
friends this it. He jumped out and came around and opened the side door
and we got out and walked over to take in the view. An enormous valley
stretched away to the right and left of us. It was unlike any valley I'd ever
seen before, as it wasn't actually a valley but rather a giant scar gouged out
of the landscape. It plunged hundreds of metres to the bottom and the sides
were terraced into roadways. On one of these across and to the left machines
that looked like giant front-end loaders were scooping up black stuff and
dumping it into the backs of enormous dump trucks. The trucks were so
big they looked ridiculous, like an absurdist inflation of a truck. Straight

across the ditch something that looked like a dragline, again an absurdly big machine, was ripping up the brown dirt at the bottom of the pit. Meanwhile, at the other end of the cut, what was obviously Wolfgang's bucket wheel excavator was chewing into a vein of coal in the vertical earth wall.

So, said Wolfgang, his sense of pride clearly apparent, here vee haff it all. He pointed at the front-end loaders, so over here we see ze truck bucket operations, gatzzering ze loose coal. And then in front of us we have ze dragline, which we are using to clear ze surface waste and expose ze coal and over there is my favourite, ze bucket wheel excavator, vich is digging out a coal seam.

Big fucker said Kevin a trace of awe in his voice.

Yes said Wolfgang, as I haff told you he said, looking at me, we haff to bring it from Germany in bits and pieces and put it together here. We stood and looked at the enormous pit for a few minutes.

You know, he went on, it is top quality coal vee are mining here. It is top grade coking coal, vich is used in blast furnaces for smelting iron ore to make steel. So vee send ze coal to Japan and they use it to make steel from ore zey haff got from Western Australia and zen zis steel is used to make those trucks you see over there. It is a nice circle. He made a wide gesture with his arm. And zere is so much coal around here vee vill be mining it for hundreds of years.

We got back into the bus and he took us back to the canteen and dropped us off. We stood around wondering what to do next. One of the giant trucks trundled past, shaking the ground in a swirl of coal dust. It was as big as a two-storey building. The tyres were huge, two or three times the height of a man and I wondered how they changed them when they got a puncture. Wolfgang had said the trucks were from Japan but when we were at school, Kevin's father, who was an engineer, had gotten me a job in the summer holidays doing maintenance work at a factory in Stanmore that made gearboxes for mining trucks, so some of these things must have been made in Australia. Not at this particular factory any more though, because it had recently closed and been demolished and a McDonalds had been built in its place.

It was too hot and dusty to stand around outside so we went back into the canteen and ordered more tea and some cupcakes. The miners had finished their breakfasts and we had the place to ourselves. A radio was playing radio pop music, *My Sharona* by The Knack. Only Alka, who had no taste, liked it: it was too commercial and derivative for the rest of us. It seemed like we'd seen all there was to see, so we went out and got into the car and went back to town.

26

There was nothing to do now that there was no more work, so Gordie and I resolved to continue our journey to Townsville the next day. Kevin elected to come with us, while Alka stayed at Moranbah with Al and Lachlan, the idea being that they would catch up with us when the painting was finished. We arranged to meet at a caravan park north of Townsville that Gordie knew about. Glen would go back to Brisbane and Louise.

That night, after we got back from our farewell visit to the pub, it began to rain. And to rain and to rain and to rain, hammering on the roof of the caravan and the canvas of the annex. Obviously there was a cyclone nearby. A few days earlier over a cup of tea Carl the drummer had told me about the great Brisbane flood of 1974. It had rained for weeks. A dozen or so people were drowned, hundreds were injured and thousands of homes and buildings were destroyed. Carl's family home was flooded, a wooden Queenslander on stilts, underneath which was a basement, which was where his drums were stored. He could laugh about it now, wading about in waist-deep water holding bits of his drum kit over his head. It was like an apocalypse he said, big ships broke loose in the Brisbane River and drifted about bumping into bridges and causing chaos. People were washed away and never seen again. I thought about all of this as I lay awake in the caravan listening to the relentless torrent of rain. How would we be able to drive through the downpour if it didn't stop by morning? Gordie snored blissfully on his bunk, untroubled by my concerns and prepared to just take things as they came: a skill for living I knew I would be better off acquiring.

Eventually, in the small hours I managed to get off to sleep. The rain didn't stop, though by morning it was less torrential, and we agreed to go anyway, rain or no rain; after all, this was Queensland in the rainy season, and it was not the last we'd see of it. I had intended to go over to the hospital to see if Maria was on duty so as to say goodbye, as apart from Carl I felt as if she was the only person in Moranbah I'd made any sort of connection with. But after tea and toast Gordie and Kevin were ready to leave, so I decided we should just go, as I hadn't gotten to know her that well anyway.

Kevin and Gordie stowed their bags in the back of the Ford and then climbed in and I performed my usual routine of checking the oil and the water and then got in myself, started up and backed away from the van. Then we exited the gates of the Coal Country Caravan Park for the last time and drove through the wet streets of the town. We went to the bottle-o and bought a carton of XXXX. I stopped at the petrol station and filled up and poured a litre of oil into the engine. We drove off and picked up the Peak Downs Highway at the end of the access road and headed towards Mackay. Not far out of town we came up to the back end of a coal train on the rail line that ran parallel to the highway. Slowly we passed the long string of open-topped grey rail wagons clattering along through the scrub in the falling rain. Mounds of black coal peaked over the top of each car, I had no idea how many of them there were, hundreds. Fuck said Kevin in amazement, as after a few minutes of whizzing along the road, we were still nowhere near the head of the train. The engine was somewhere up ahead though, because we could hear the long sonorous wail of its horn, sounding especially mournful through the mist and rain. A little further on we passed the three grimy diesels that were pulling the load to the coal terminal on the coast.

We left the coal train behind and continued down the highway as the rain began to ease. Soon it stopped all together. Up ahead I could see a long line of traffic halted on the highway. I pulled up behind it. We got out. Two thin men in singlets and shorts were standing next to the truck stopped ahead of us talking. What's goin' on I asked? They turned towards us and one of them, after glancing at our NSW number plates, said dismissively, Creek's flooded. He spoke in the remarkable way Queenslanders had of barely opening their perpetually close-lipped mouths as they talked. Let's go and have look said Gordie, heading over to the back of the wagon and opening the tailgate. He pulled out a XXXX and then fished around for a bottle opener and his foam stubby holder. He inserted the squat bottle into the foam receptacle, knocked the top off, and took a long swig. He gazed in my direction, What are you lookin' at he said, the sun's over the yardarm. Is it? I answered, I can't tell, it's too cloudy.

We walked past a long line of vehicles, trucks, utes, 4WDs, Holdens and Fords, a few Japanese sedans, farm vehicles, a bus, even a petrol tanker, all of them settled on the tarmac still wet from the rain, most of them empty of drivers and passengers. As we rounded a slight bend we could see a crowd of people up ahead clustered in the middle of the road. They were watching the action at the point where the bitumen plunged into a torrent of water. A sign said Denison Creek, behind which a mass of swirling grey water surged past. It hardly equated with my idea of a creek, more like a raging river, the floodwaters surging up the sides of the embankment and over the line of scrub bordering the watercourse. Out in the middle of the flood sat a Toyota 4WD ute, stuck on the bridge which obviously sat somewhere below the waterline.

A fat Queensland policeman, the buttons on his light blue shirt straining over his belly, his dark blue shorts bunched under it, stood gazing out at the trapped vehicle. Gordie went up and stood behind him and, holding his beer in his left hand, proceeded to give him the finger behind his back with his right hand, which drew a few chuckles from some of the onlookers. A big Komatsu front-end loader was pulled up facing the water. The cop turned to the man next to him, a thick-set bloke in grey shorts and a faded blue singlet, with a long length of rope curled on his shoulder. You right Nev?, asked the cop. He mumbled an affirmative reply. Alright, give it a go then, said the cop.

'Nev' waded out into the water, rope on his shoulder, and proceeded to walk across the submerged road bridge to the stricken vehicle, the water surging around his tree trunk-like legs. When he got to the Toyota he looped the rope around the bull bar on the front and tied it on. Another man,

94

obviously the owner, followed him out and tugged the driver's door open and climbed inside. After checking the strength of his knot Nev turned and, holding the other end of the rope headed back towards us. Once he'd emerged from the water, he fastened the rope to the front arm of the earth mover and then, water dripping from his shorts, climbed up into the cab and started the engine. The cop looked up and gave him a nod and then gave the driver out in the ute a thumbs up sign. Its engine straining, the big yellow machine began to move backwards, as the rope tightened and pulled the Toyota towards us, the driver steering towards the point where the road dipped into the water. As the ute was pulled up the bank, looking like the losing end of a tug o' war contest, the onlookers cheered and clapped, and then, the fun over, many began to drift back towards their own vehicles. The water level was dropping now, but we would all still need to wait another half hour or so before it was safe enough to cross. Nev climbed down from his cab and we walked back to the car. Gordie pulled his now empty stubby out of the holder and reached for another. Kevin and I took one each too. We sat down on the road at the back of the car and clinked our bottles together. Here's to Queensland, I said. A land of droughts and flooding rains, said Kevin, who'd always been one for poetry.

Before too long the vehicles close to the water began to start up and move off, so we finished our beers, got into the Ford, and followed them. You could see the wooden bridge now, the rushing water lapping just under it, the fat policeman standing to the side and overseeing the orderly progression of the traffic under the grey, heavy-clouded sky.

We took our turn to cross over and then kept heading towards the coast, bypassing Mackay, a town we weren't interested in, and taking some back-roads that linked us up with the Bruce Highway. We stopped at a roadhouse and ate hamburgers, not sure if this was our lunch or tea.

The hold-up at the flooded creek meant that it was getting late and that we needed to stop for the night somewhere south of Townsville. When we reached the twin towns of Ayr and Home Hill, at the mouth of the Burdekin River, we decided to call a halt for the day. We passed a bowling club and thought that it would be a good place to sleep. It was after midnight so there was no one around. We parked and got out our sleeping bags and went around the back of the club to the verandah overlooking the greens. There was a cane toad sitting facing the wall of the building and every now and then it would leap forward and bang against the fibro wall, only to fall back to the spot it had started from. Splat; splat; splat against the wall. It was an absolutely pointless activity. Gordie walked up and kicked it, spinning it around. It hopped off in the other direction, away from the wall and out onto the bowling green. Maybe it was blind, I knew nothing about cane toads. In fact, it was the first one I'd ever seen.

Mosquitos were buzzing around us as we unrolled our sleeping bags and crawled into them. I tried to get to sleep amongst the buzzing, having to swat at my face repeatedly. They were eating us alive. Fuck this said Gordie after a few minutes, these mozzies are bullshit. We had a can of Aerogard in the car, so I said we should go and get into the car and spray the repellent. We got up and rolled up our sleeping bags and walked back around to the front of the club pursued by the biggest, most aggressive mozzies I'd ever encountered. We got into the car and a cloud of them swarmed in with us and continued their attack. I sprayed the can of Aerogard until we were choking on the noxious fumes, and eventually they seemed to go away. So Gordie and I had to sleep sitting up while Kevin got to lie down on the back seat. I was too tired to care. I fell asleep thinking about the cane toad. Banging against the solid wall like that it seemed the perfect metaphor for existence up here. Every day, like Sisyphus, the Queenslanders pushed the big boulder up the hill, and then the floodwaters washed it back down again.

27

I woke up at dawn with my lungs burning from the insecticide. The sky was still crowded with big grey clouds. No rain was falling, though there was lots of mist in the air. To the right of the bowling club was the most tropical scene I'd ever looked on: a row of tall, extremely skinny palm trees standing along the edge of a small bush-fringed watercourse. Everything was lush and green. I opened the car door and climbed out to get some fresh air. I breathed in deep lungfuls, there was a delicious fresh dampness to the clean air.

After we'd all had a piss against the palm trees we drove up the highway towards Townsville. The clouds began to break up and the sun came out, illuminating the countryside in that beautiful crisp and sparkling way you get after rain has cleared the air. We drove on up the sunlit highway through the fields of cattle and cane that Grant McLennan would sing about a few years later. Townsville had been the goal of our journey since we set out but as we passed through the outlying suburbs I realised that we had no idea, now that we were here, what to do in this place. Gordie intended to link up with the friends of his friends who lived here but he wanted to leave this for a few days. He'd never been to Townsville before but because he'd paid such close attention to the stories and conversations of his mates back home who knew the place, he knew the sort of things about the city that only a local would know. He suggested that we go the cafeteria at the Coles supermarket for breakfast. This seemed a good idea, so we drove into the centre of town and parked the car. The cafeteria was on the floor above the main market hall of the Coles store. In those days Coles and Woolworths were not just food stores but carried a much wider range of consumer goods. We walked up the stairs and went to the counter. I hadn't had much to eat for a few days so I ordered the full breakfast – eggs, bacon, sausages, fried mushrooms and toast – and washed down with a nice pot of tea it was absolutely excellent.

On the way out we bought a box of mosquito coils – horrible, noxious curly little things made in Indonesia – which the previous night's experience had taught us would be invaluable from now on.

With breakfast accomplished we were back in the position of not knowing what to do next. We walked around the pedestrian mall and the main street and gazed up at a round building that looked like a giant lipstick. Gordie said it was called the Sugar Shaker and that that was what it was supposed to represent, not a lipstick. Given the amount of sugar cane we'd seen in the last couple of days this made some sense. I knew absolutely nothing about Townsville and was surprised to see that it sat at the base of a big mountain, Castle Hill. Let's go up there I said. This was sort of a compulsion on my part. Whenever I went to somewhere new, I had a young man's burning desire to ascend to the highest point (if there was one) and lord it over the landscape. This was obviously the sort of male impulse that had propelled European men across the globe over the previous centuries to take mental and physical possession of other people's homes (leading to the creation of places like Townsville). The best example I can think of is, 'Light's Vision', the statue of Colonel Light on Montefiore Hill in Adelaide.

For me this urge would be fully satisfied a few years later, when, as a backpacker I went to Bologna in Italy. In the 12th century the powerful men of Bologna were obsessed with building hundreds of tall brick towers as demonstrations of their wealth and strength. Some of these towers, hundreds of metres high, are still standing and tourists can ascend them and observe the intricacies of the medieval city laid out below.

There was nothing medieval about the view of Townsville from Castle Hill. No doubt there was a much older history than a medieval one down there, of which there was little trace left, now that the Indigenous people had been driven out by the European Invasion. Now the view was of what was left of a colonial town centre – late nineteenth, early twentieth century – most of which had been demolished and replaced with modern monuments like the Sugar Shaker, and around this centre lay a sprawl of suburbs reaching out to the coast and along a long, curved beach. Off the coast was the green lump of Magnetic Island, so named because it apparently upset Captain Cook's compass when he sailed past naming things in 1770.

It was a hot and humid morning, even on top of this big and pitiless lump of granite, and we walked around shirtless in our shorts and thongs. Still, after weeks at ground level in Moranbah it was nice to get some space and some air.

Gordie knew of a caravan park, the Currambeena, north of town, which was where we intended to stay. So we got back into the car and drove out of the hilltop car park and headed back down to town, driving over to the north side and picking up the highway again. We came to a supermarket and stopped to get some essentials, eggs, bread, butter, tea and so on, then continued on our way. A few kilometres out of town the road went up another hill and at the crest there was a roadside lookout point gesturing to the country to the north, so I pulled over and we got out, and sat down on some rocks to take in the view. On the other side of the flat land out in front of us sat a massive jumble of pipes, chimneys and various arrangements of metal. Yellow smoke was rising from the chimneys.

Indeed, a massive yellow cloud was hanging over the entire valley. Yabulu, said Gordie, chuckling. It's a nickel smelter. Fuckin great eh. You can smell it! And it was true, there was a noticeable sour stench in the air. Yabulu meant place of grass in the language of the people whose land it had been before the Invasion, but if there was any grass still down there amongst the toxin and the poison, then it would have to be hardy stuff. Indeed, if there were any Aborigines still down there, they would need to be hardy too. Gordie, with his punk ethic, in which there was no future and everything was understood to be a swindle, seemed to delight in this total desecration of the landscape, this industrial poisoning on a grand scale. After the way the landscape had been ripped apart and torn up back at Moranbah this damaged vista came as no great surprise to me. This was just business as usual, and the people responsible for what we were seeing and smelling weren't punks with an appetite for destruction, they were businessmen with an appetite for money.

28

On the way up the highway we passed through a small village with the marvellous name of Rollingstone. It seemed so quaintly exotic and I wondered why places in New South Wales didn't have such great names. The most substantial structure in Rollingstone was the pub, which was quite big, and destined to play a key role in our time in the area. Another ten or so kilometres and we came to the Currumbeena Caravan Park. It was off the road to the right, a flat expanse of grass with vans dotted here and there, nothing like the cheek-to-cheek urban crowding of Moranbah. I turned into the gateway and breathed a sigh of relief at having reached another aimed-for destination.

Gordie and I went into the office. The park was run by a man and woman about ten years older than us, who seemed to be pretty casual about the whole thing. They gave us the key to a van in the centre of the park: an off-white, mid-range Chesney with an annex, just like at Moranbah, with room for the others once they arrived. We drove over, parked next to it, went inside and put the electric kettle on. We took the foldup chairs from the annex outside and sat in them drinking our tea and looking out across the prosaic field of caravans glinting in the afternoon sun.

It didn't require much discussion to decide that our best course of action would be to go down to the hotel at Rollingstone for the evening. We pulled into the car park just as night was falling. It always amazed me how quickly it got dark in the tropics: no twilight, then suddenly, in what seemed a few minutes, the day had gone and the dark night was all around. The lights were on in the pub. It was a beautiful wooden Nineteen Twenties or Thirties structure, filled no doubt with XXXX. We walked up the front steps and went inside, into the bistro. We hadn't had anything to eat since our breakfast at Coles cafeteria so we all ordered steak: t-bones with chips. Kevin went to the bar and ordered a round of pots. The steaks were great. There was a jukebox playing The Saints; they were Queenslanders after all. And at the far end of the room was a pool table. We were happy here; it would have been hard to think how things could have been designed to suit us better. We finished our meals and went over to the pool table, which was covered in the rarely seen red baize rather than green. Kevin and Gordie took the first game and I would play the winner. Next to the table two big glass doors opened out onto a verandah, so I stepped outside. It was a beautiful, warm tropical night: the sky behind the palms in the hotel garden was a rich purple velvet. I looked down, and sitting on the wooden slats of the verandah floor, was a big, round, shiny black beetle. It was five or six centimeters long with two large horns on its head: just sitting there minding its own business. I knew it must be a rhinoceros beetle, though I'd never seen one before. As with cane toads, I knew nothing about rhinoceros beetles. I observed it for a while, reasoning that if I left it alone it would leave me alone.

I went back inside. Gordie was having an off night and Kevin was carving him up; he was already onto the black, which he potted with reckless confidence, so much so that the cue ball bounced back across the table and into the side pocket, giving the game to Gordie. I fished a twenty-cent piece out of my pocket and put it in the table. Gordie racked up the balls as they dropped out and I took the cue from Kevin and chalked the end with the block of chalk dangling from the piece of string at the end of the table. Gordie broke, and the balls scattered and a large one went down. He smirked and stepped over to pot another, but missed with his next. Now it was my turn. I always preferred the small anyway and they were well spaced around the table. I sunk one, and then the next and the next. I was on a roll much like Kevin must have been, and I shot without pausing, just lined them up and sank them. I sank another three in quick succession, and then I was on the black. I stopped for a moment and chalked my cue again. It was a simple shot, straight into a corner pocket. I took my time and lined it up, but I had lost the fluid confidence of my previous run. As I drew the cue back and then pushed it forward I could feel the uncertainty running through my arm from one end to the other. The cue ball hit the black with a soft crack and then followed it on and fell into the pocket after it. Gordie had won again! He smirked and said You cunts are hopeless, and added Go and get another round, it's your shout.

As I went to the bar I thought about what had just happened. It was always my Achilles heel when it came to pool: I could play brilliant shots just by lining them up and shooting without hesitation, but as soon as I paused to concentrate, my skills seemed to disappear. When a shot really mattered and I took my time, my smoothness fell away and I generally messed up. Why was this? Many years later I would find a story by Heinrich von Kleist, *Über das Marionettetheater* (On the Marionette Theatre), which provided an explanation. It is 1801 and the narrator meets a friend who is a highly acclaimed dancer at a puppet show and they fall to pondering how it is that truly good puppeteers can make their marionettes move so smoothly and gracefully, like the best dancers. The friend's conclusion is that it all depends on being spontaneous, and acting without thinking too much about what one is doing. For, he argues, when self-consciousness arises in relation to an action, one is no longer embodied in the actual physical act, but is examining it from the outside, and so the possibility of fluid, seamless action is replaced by concern and hesitancy. I bought the three pots of beer and took them back to the table.

Kevin and Gordie were playing another game. Gordie was winning easily and I marvelled over the way some people always seemed to have the odds in their favour, while others, like Kevin, always had them against them. We continued with this round robin – the winner playing the one who sat out – for the rest of the night. When the pub closed, drunker than anyone in charge of a motor vehicle should have been, I drove us back to our caravan and crashed out.

29

The next morning we woke up late. Now that we had a fixed address Gordie wanted to go into Townsville and register for the dole. I thought I might as well do this too, and Kevin needed to transfer his Sickness Benefits payments. We parked the car and went into the Commonwealth Employment Service office, at which you needed to register in order to get a form to take to the Department of Social Security, which paid you the Unemployment Benefits. After registering our names at the front counter we sat down in the waiting room. A half dozen or so very casually dressed people were scanning the job descriptions displayed on the green notice boards in front of us. A clean cut man about thirty years old, in a short-sleeved light blue business shirt tucked into beige shorts partnered with brown shoes and long white socks called my name and led me to a desk where we sat down. Little did I know I would be going through this very same routine myself in a couple of years' time, when *I* would be working at the CES office in Bondi Junction. If I'd been able to tell him this he would have been impressed, though of course I couldn't, as I had no idea what direction my life was going to go in from here. He *was* impressed though that I'd actually been working in Moranbah but wanted to know what I was going to do now that I was in Townsville. I told him I didn't know, and that I worked mostly as a waiter or bartender. He accepted this, even though I had long unkempt hair and a scraggly beard, and he registered me in the CES system as a hospitality worker, even though I couldn't imagine any manager hiring me in my current state. He signed off on the Social Security form and wished me all the best and I went back out to the waiting room to sit with Kevin and wait for Gordie. He wasn't much longer than me and we left, without bothering to look at the jobs on the boards.

The DSS was on the pedestrian mall. Gordie and I handed in our forms and showed our ID but Kevin needed an interview. So Gordie and I went outside to wait for him. We sat down on the ledge that ran around a water feature. The ground was littered with cigarette butts. It was hot and humid, the sky pale and hazy. A group of seagulls were fighting over some discarded chips, squawking and pecking at each other.

Kevin came out after about ten minutes. What happened? I asked. They transferred my benefit he said. Good, so now we could get on with things. Gordie wanted to go and see the friends of his friends, three brothers called Tannenbaum. He had an address for them, so we left the seagulls to their chips and went and got the car and drove to the suburb of North Ward, which was next to a beach quite close to the city centre. We stopped outside a rambling old Queenslander that was in need of a coat of paint. There was a dirt-covered Nissan 4WD sitting in the driveway; a few rusting car and motorbike parts littered the overgrown lawn. We got out and went up to the front door. Gordie rang the bell and then rapped on the door for good measure. A young man with short sandy hair and a long beard with a quizzical look on his face opened the door. He was a few years older than us. Gordie introduced himself and then us. He invited us in. Do youse wanna cuppa tea? he asked and ushered us into the loungeroom. We said yes and sat down.

The brothers were called Karl, Hans and Peter. This one was Hans. The other two were visiting their mother. Hans hadn't gone with them because she gave him the shits he told us with a grin. Anyway someone had to feed the dogs, which is what he had been just about to do when we knocked on the door. He got up and went back to the kitchen to make our tea. Gordie followed him. I looked around the room, the foam was escaping from a split in the lounge Kevin was sitting on and there was an Iggy Pop poster on the wall, the picture from the cover of *Raw Power* where he is shirtless and looks like some kind of petulant orange space alien. I stared at it, until they came back in with our mugs of tea. Gordie and Hans talked about the people they knew, primarily Gordie's best friend, Dave Smithton, a total low-life drug addict as far as I was concerned. He'd lived here with the brothers and even worked with them. The Tannenbaums ran a tree-killing business. Farmers employed them on land that they wanted cleared. And so, armed with axes and a carload of poison the brothers would set about poisoning every tree in sight, in preparation for the bulldozers. Gordie thought this was a great punk way to make a living.

Hans said he wanted to feed the dogs and got up and went into the kitchen. We followed him in there and he opened the fridge and pulled out a plastic bag full of meat. We all went out into the backyard and a black bull terrier, obviously Hans' dog, ran up to him and licked his leg. He laughed, good boy Satan he said and ruffled the top of his head. Further back in the yard a blue cattle dog and an odd looking brown dog with an irregular line of hair running down its back, stood and snarled at us. Hans pulled a red lump of meat out of the bag and threw it in front of Satan. The other two ran forward and he began to throw meat to them too. What sorta meat is that? asked Gordie. Mostly roo answered Hans. What sort of dog is that I asked pointing at the brown dog. Ruben's a bull terrier Rhodesian Ridge-back cross, he said. This seemed like a pretty serious sort of dog to me. As well as a large cage for the dogs the backyard also contained a barbeque and a wooden table, along with a number of mangy palm trees.

The dogs chewed ferociously on the meat and bones and we left them to it and went back into the house. As Karl and Peter wouldn't be back for a few hours we agreed that we should come back on Saturday when they would all be home. This was fine with us, so we went out and got into the car and drove back up to the caravan, stopping at the pub for a beer, since we were going straight past.

30

The next day we had baked beans and fried eggs on toast for breakfast. Another person Gordie knew was an ex-Sydney drug addict called Charlie Varafakis. He lived at a place called Hidden Valley, which was on the other side of the mountain range to the west. We decided to drive over and visit him.

A winding road led off the highway and up to a town called Paluma. Apparently there was a dam nearby from which Townsville's water was sourced. We climbed ever higher up the hillsides without encountering much passing traffic. Eventually the road ran alongside a fast flowing creek and soon we came to a beautiful old stone bridge across the creek. It was an idyllic spot, rainforest all around, and I stopped the car and we got out. A big black swastika had been spray painted on the low sandstone bridge wall facing the road, along with the name D. Voss in large capitals. This was also someone we knew: Dave Voss, another member of the drug scene. Gordie was ecstatic at the sight of this punk act of defilement, and demanded that I take his picture. I had a small Kodak camera that I sometimes used in the back of the car and I went over to get it, while Gordie grabbed his props. In his sleeveless Sex Pistols t-shirt and with his perpetual stubby in its polystyrene holder he squatted down next to the swastika, beer in one hand and his knife in the other. He took a big swig of beer and spurted it out of his mouth in a long stream. I was getting a bit tired of this punk silliness. I really didn't like this act of vandalism and desecration of the beautiful little bridge. I could see how people who lived in miserable English cities under Mrs. Thatcher's rule would want to embrace the punk ethic but in tropical Australia it seemed a bit puerile. Still, I really liked the music. But also, it was ok for me to criticise the lack of respect shown to this lovely

European-style stone bridge, but the Indigenous people whose land this was before the European Invasion would have viewed the putting through of the road and the building of the bridge as a desecration. It was complicated, so I ignored my annoyance and pressed the shutter so as to capture Gordie's performance on film.

A stream of clear, pure-looking water ran under the bridge and fell into a small waterfall dropping into a pristine pool. It was too beautiful to get back in the car and just leave and we stepped away from the road to look around. A big, flourishing old mango tree grew next to the bridge and there were rotting and decomposing mangoes all over the ground. I was thinking about another photo when I heard a thwack sound and dropped my camera away from my face. You cunt Gordie said, the right side of his face covered in decaying mango. Kevin had hit him fair in the head with a squishy, rotting mango. Gordie bent down and picked up a mango himself and threw it at Kevin. It hit him in the belly: he was a big target and was hard to miss. With a mischievous grin Gordie picked up another mango and threw it at me. I ducked and it missed, so I picked one up and hurled it back at him, it hit his chest, splattering across the Queen's blacked-out face on his shirt. Kevin meanwhile had thrown a few more at both of us, and it quickly turned into an every man for himself battle. Gordie scurried towards the gully walls of the creek to find some cover, but both Kevin and I managed to pick him off, in between landing bulls-eye shots on each other.

There seemed to be an inexhaustible supply of dead and dying mangoes around us so the fight continued until we got tired of it after about twenty minutes. By this point the three of us were completely covered in mushy orange mango flesh, but as I only had on a pair of shorts and no shirt I wasn't bothered. We dived into the pool under the waterfall, splashing about and diving under the water to wash the soggy vegetable matter out of our hair and off our bodies and clothes.

We climbed out of the pool and sat on a rock next to the creek to dry out. It was still hot, even up here in the hills, so we were ready to go before too long. The road continued uphill towards Paluma. As we got to the top of the range the air began to become cool and misty, and by the time we reached Paluma we were in the midst of a thick fog. Only Pommies can live here Gordie said with a laugh, 'cause it's always foggy. It was a small town of mostly wooden buildings and we continued on along the main street and out the other side, where the road began to descend again. We were soon down out of the fog and back into the verdant green landscape again.

Hidden or not, Hidden Valley wasn't too hard to find as we came to an expanse of rolling, green grassy ground at the bottom of the range. Gum trees and corrugated iron and timber shacks were dotted here and there. On a cream weatherboard building was a sign that said Post Office 4073. I was just about to suggest that we go in there and ask them where to find Charlie when Gordie shouted, There he is, and pointed to the left. A very skinny, brown-skinned, bearded fellow in a disintegrating pair of grey shorts stood surrounded by a group of chickens furiously pecking at the ground as he flung food scraps toward them. We drove up and parked next to the small timber shack that was either his home or the chook shed. He looked at us with suspicion. Gordie jumped out and said G'day Charlie. He gave a relieved smile. G'day, ya can never be too careful, he said, eyeing Kevin and myself.

Cuppa tea he said after the introductions, more as a statement than a question. Bewdy replied Gordie. He put down the chook slops bucket and led us over to his shack. The interior was just one room, like the huts, I imagined, in which the European colonists had lived in the nineteenth century. There was an old wooden table with four chairs under the one window and a primus stove in the corner.

He set some mugs of tea down on the table for us and apologised that there was no milk because he had no fridge. I hated black tea so I spooned a few teaspoons of sugar into mine. We talked about what we'd been doing and what had brought us here, about Townsville, and about life back in Sydney. He looked vacantly at each of us without blinking, and I thought of the 'thousand yard stare' that American Marines who'd seen too much combat against the Japanese in the Pacific War had been said to possess.

Still, while he was odd, he was nice enough. He went over to a cupboard next to his cooker, took out a bong and filled it with water, bringing it back to the table along with a bag of heads. He broke the heads into a bowl and rubbed them down, packed the cone, lit it with his lighter and pulled it. He pushed the bong and the bowl to Gordie. I went next. It was good stuff. Did you grow this? I asked. Yeah, he replied, it's not bad eh? Kevin had his turn and we sat around looking at each other and smiling. I need to finish feedin' the chooks, said Charlie and we all got up and went outside. It was idyllic, the afternoon sun slanting across the low hills on the other side of the valley, and it was totally quiet, apart from the sound of honeyeaters warbling in the trees.

Here and there people were moving around outside their shacks, tending their gardens and animals. Do youse wanna stay the night? asked Charlie. No thanks, shot back Gordie, we've gotta go and see the Tannenbaums tomorra mornin'. Charlie grinned at the mention of the name. Tell 'em I said hello. It was fine by me that Gordie had shut Charlie's invitation down so swiftly. As nice as it was here, I had no desire to spend the night on the floor of his shack.

He's mad, see that look in his eye, said Gordie as we drove away, that's what comes from spendin' too much time on your own. Yeah, agreed Kevin. We drove back up to Paluma and down across the bridge and back down to the coast, and never saw Hidden Valley again. A few decades later I heard that developers found Hidden Valley and built an Eco Lodge for tourists there.

31

We were too tired after our big day out to go to the pub so we just had a couple of quiet stubbies once we got back to the caravan.

The next morning we went back to see the Tannenbaums. The other two were home this time: Peter was the same age as Hans, they were twins, and Karl was a few years younger, about our age. So we went in and Hans again made us tea. We were standing in the kitchen talking when at the end of the hallway an Aboriginal man came to the front door. Karl called out G'day Lucky, come in. He replied Owyagoin, and came through the door and went into the front room on the right. We finished our tea and the brothers drifted out into the backyard; Gordie, keen to ingratiate himself, followed them.

I'd left my wallet in the car and I didn't want to leave it sitting out there in the street, so I went to get it. I glanced into the front room and the man called Lucky was sitting on the side of the bed. I went out to grab the wallet, and looked into the room again on my way in. He was sitting on the bed and nodded hello to me in a way that indicated he was interested in me, so I went in and sat down on the bed too.

He was probably about thirty years old and had the blackest skin I had ever seen, and was wearing jeans, cowboy boots, a purple shirt, a brown blazer and a black Stetson hat. We sat there looking at each other for a minute or two. I had never really met any Aborigines before, as there had not been any living in the area where I grew up, although I knew that there, on the eastern side of Botany Bay, within sight of Cook's landing place, there had been lots of Aborigines around before the British invaded. I remember my Year 3 primary school teacher, a sweet young woman who would play us *The Seekers*, telling the class You won't have to worry about Aborigines when you grow up because they will have all died out by then. Well here I was grown up, and Lucky did not appear to have died out. But I really didn't know what to say to him or talk to him about. He didn't say anything to me either, just sat there looking at me, thinking I don't know what.

Eventually I asked him, for want of anything better to say, Are you from Townsville? No, he said, and after a moment's silence added, I'm from Charters Towers. Uh-huh, I said; I knew that this was a town inland from Townsville, but I knew nothing about it, so I couldn't think of anything else to say. We sat there in silence, me not knowing how to communicate with him or what to communicate about. We were both Australians, but our experiences of the country had been so radically different that he may well have been from another planet, so little did I understand what his life must be like. The one thing that really struck me was how black his skin was: he was completely unlike anyone I'd ever met before.

Still, we spoke a language we could both understand, but all I could do in the way of conversation was to interrogate him. How do you know the Tannenbaums? I asked. I was workin' on a property out at Torrens Creek, he said, and they come out there killin' trees. I got to know 'em then. Now when I'm in town I come and see 'em.

I could hear the sound of heavy feet thudding up the hallway and Kevin appeared in the doorway of the room. You want to come and have a beer mate? he asked. Sure I said, and stood up from the bed. Nice to meet you Lucky, I said and nodded, and went out after Kevin, leaving him there still sitting quietly on the bed.

We sat in the backyard drinking our beers under the shade of Alexander palms. Gordie was getting on like a house on fire with the Tannenbaums, laughing at all their jokes and slipping in his own sarcastic comments when there was a chance. I wasn't saying much, I wasn't keen to suck up to them, I didn't think too much of tree killing as a profession. Kevin meanwhile added the occasional Yeah mate in polite agreement but he was pretty quiet too, his shyness and self-consciousness meant he didn't like drawing atten-tion to himself in unfamiliar situations. The dogs ran around on the grass growling at each other now and then. None of the brothers seemed too bothered about what Lucky was up to, it seemed they were quite used to his calm, silent presence.

It got to lunchtime and since no one had offered us anything other than beer I said we should make tracks, with Gordie saying we'd come back in a few days. We got up to go out to the car. I said goodbye to Lucky who was still sitting on his own in the front room. There was a fish n' chip shop down the street so we went and bought some pieces of fish and some chips and went down to the park along the waterfront and sat on the grass and ate our lunch and had another beer. It was beautiful looking out at Magnetic Island on a perfect sunny afternoon and it would have been nice to go in for a swim but there were box jellyfish to worry about, which even the normally reckless Gordie wasn't prepared to risk.

32

We got back to the caravan in time for afternoon tea. Some previous occupant had left behind an old cricket bat and ball, so we set up the garbage bin as a wicket and commenced a game of tip and run. This filled in the hours until it was time to go down to the pub.

Kevin and Gordie were playing pool and I was sitting out. I was thinking that I hadn't talked to my parents for a long time. There was a public telephone outside the pub. I got up and said I'm goin' to ring up my Mum and Dad and went out. The glass phone box was glowing in its neon brightness on the other side of the pub's car park. I walked down the front steps and across the gravel and hard dirt surface. I approached the phone box from the side and just as I got close to it my feet suddenly stepped into air and I dropped into a big hole, landing on the bottom, shouting out FUCK! and twisting my right knee as I landed. It was so dark in the car park I hadn't been able to see the hole. The four beers I'd had probably hadn't helped. I clambered out: there was a big pile of dirt next to the hole illuminated by the light from the phone box, but no warning sign or safety barrier. This seemed typical of the She'll Be Right attitude that seemed to rule Queensland I thought. I hobbled to the phone box, my knee throbbing, pulled open the door and stepped inside. A lovely little green gecko was attached to the glass side of the cabinet, and the beauty of its delicate suction cup fingers and toes made me forget the pain in my leg. I put a couple of dollar coins into the phone and dialed our number. My father answered. Everything was business as usual at home, he and Mum were well and Aunt Millie was too, though they all missed me he said, especially Snowy the dog. Be careful he said; I didn't tell him anything about having just fallen down a hole.

I limped back across the car park and up the steps and back into the pub. They were still playing pool. I told them what had happened and they both laughed. I felt annoyed and stupid for having let such a dumb thing happen. I had a bit of a headache from having been drinking earlier in the day and I was in no mood to play pool and drink more beer. I suggested we go home and, amazingly, they agreed.

I took some codeine to help me sleep with the pain in my knee, but I tossed and turned with it throughout the humid night. It still hurt when I got out of bed in the morning and I thought I might feel better if I went to the amenities block and had a cool shower. It was on the other side of the park, but as I walked across the grass my knee began to feel better. This was good because there was such a swarm of mosquitos in the shower block I gave up on the idea of a shower and went back to the caravan.

I put the kettle on and sat down at the little kitchenette table. I'd bought a newspaper, *The Courier Mail*, at the fish n' chip shop but hadn't had time to look at it yet. I began to peruse it. I hadn't read a paper in weeks. President Ronald Reagan had met with the families of the hostages who had been held captive in the American embassy in Tehran. The Pope said that freedom consists not in doing what we like, but in having the right to do what we should; it was assumed he was referring to the Solidarity movement that was opposing the communist government in his homeland, Poland. The kettle boiled and I got up and put a tea bag into a mug and poured in some hot water. Then I got the milk out of the fridge, splashed some into the tea and sat back down with the paper. In the Northern Territory an inquest was being held into the disappearance at Ayres Rock of the baby girl Azaria Chamberlain. As everyone knew, her mother Lindy maintained that a dingo had taken her daughter. I turned to the sports pages. In cricket, Australia had beaten New Zealand again, in the final of the one-day international competition, and this time we hadn't even needed any underarm bowling. Kevin came in from the annex, made himself a cup of tea, and sat down with me. We laughed about the cricket. He asked if he could have the crossword and I handed the newspaper over to him.

33

We settled into a lazy routine for the next couple of weeks. Taking it easy in the mornings, poking around the local area a bit later, having a hit with the cricket bat, going in to Townsville, and going down to the pub most nights. A few kilometres along on the way to Townsville the road crossed a concrete bridge over a watercourse. It was as wide as a river but as was often the case up here the sign said Creek. One afternoon on the way back from town I stopped the car and we walked out onto the bridge for a look. We stood at the railing that ran along the side of the bridge and looked over. It was about twenty metres down to the placid water; upstream a kilometre or so the water disappeared into a clump of trees. Without saying anything Gordie took off his glasses and t-shirt and put them down, stepped out of his thongs and climbed over the rail. Then he leapt off the edge of the bridge and plummeted straight down into the water, landing in a big splash and disappearing under the surface. Kevin and I peered over waiting for him to come to the surface. He popped up and shouted That was fucken Gas. As he swam towards the shore Kevin pulled off his own shirt and leapt out into space, giving out a Tarzan yell as he plummeted. As I watched his corpulent form bob around on the water I reasoned it must be safe enough if he hadn't hit the bottom, so I took my own thongs off and let go of the rail. It felt like stepping off the second floor of a building, but the rush was so powerful it blotted out the fear, something like a roller coaster.

So we spent an hour or so continuing to jump off the bridge, swim to the shore and walk back up and jump off again. When I think about it now I find it hard to understand how it was that we never encountered any police or other authority figures as we roamed the countryside doing basically whatever we liked. It was as if the Queensland landscape was a big, adult-sized playground in which we drifted about amusing ourselves, fuelled by beer and whatever drugs came to hand. European men had been behaving like this in Australia for two centuries now. And we were reaping the rewards. Back at Big Hill, Robert the ABC announcer had said that I hadn't been living the life of a bank clerk, and he was certainly right. But someone had worked to provide all the elements of this landscape for us: someone had killed or rounded up and institutionalised the Indigenous owners, cleared the land of trees, ripped all the minerals out of the ground and built all the roads and railways and buildings so that we could have a space to have our reckless, irresponsible fun. And these people were closer to us than we realised or understood: we actually knew the people who killed the trees: the Tannenbaums and men like them. And so with everything taken care of for us, we continued to thoughtlessly enjoy ourselves.

One afternoon we were out in front of the caravan playing cricket when a familiar white Holden panel van drove across the grassy space of the park and pulled up next to us, with Al, Lachlan and Alka grinning on the front seat. Tess was in the back. They clambered out. The painting was finished, so here they were. What else was there to do now apart from put the kettle on, have a cuppa and then go down to the pub.

34

The next morning we all went in to Townsville so that Al and Lachlan could register for the dole. Gordie, Kevin, Alka and I sat waiting for them on benches in the Mall. There was an envelope on the ground in front of me, and I idly picked it up and opened it. There was a twenty-dollar bill inside. Twenty dollars was a lot of money. Once when I had been working as a waiter in the Members' bar of Randwick Racecourse the knockabout entrepreneur John Singleton had tipped me twenty dollars after his horse won, and I'd felt as if I was rich. Look at this I said, holding up the twenty. I'll have that said Gordie, and snatched it from my hand. Bewdy, he crowed, Let's get a carton of XXXX and a kilo o' prawns! I was annoyed that he taken it off me as I'd thought that we could spend it on petrol, but this seemed a celebratory sort of alternative so I said ok.

After Lachlan and Al came out of the Social Security office we drove to the fish market to buy the prawns, and then stopped at the pub at Rollingstone for a carton of beer. Then it was back to the caravan where we sat around the table in the annex and drank the stubbies and peeled and ate the prawns. My father had grown up on the water and instilled in me a love of seafood from a young age. I remembered that when I was a child he would take me to Georges River, near where he had lived as a boy, and we would prise fresh oysters off the rocks with his oyster knife and eat them. One time when we were fishing off a jetty we caught a big crab and it impaled his thumb on one of its pincers and I had to cut the pincer off with our fishing knife before it would let go. He was really annoyed with me that in the panic of the situation I had then thrown the claw into the water rather than saving it to eat. So anyway, I loved prawns and I was happy to consume them on a hot afternoon and wash them down with beer. So were

Al, Lachlan and Alka, after the tedium of Moranbah, where they had not had anything very interesting to eat over the past couple of weeks, and from which they brought no news, nothing much having happened since we left.

We still hadn't paid any rent for our caravan. The people who ran the place hadn't asked for any, and we weren't very happy that the mozzies in the amenities block made it unuseable, which was something they couldn't seem to be bothered to do anything about. So we didn't bother them and they didn't bother us. One night as we were sitting around having a few beers a Holden station wagon stopped next to our van. In it was yet another drug scene acquaintance, a bloke named Alasdair, known to everyone as Jack from Nabiac: a rural town on the mid north coast of New South Wales, which is where he was originally from. His girlfriend Helena was with him, along with her 4-year-old son, Jason. I'd never met Jack before but he was well known to Gordie and to Lachlan. He was also a friend of the Tannenbaums who had told him we were in the area. He asked if they could stay with us and we said sure, why not? He was in his early twenties with unruly curly brown hair. He had a large scar on his forehead. Apparently when he had been living in Townsville two years previously, one dark night he had been driving his car down a street that ended in a concrete culvert. There had been no streetlights and no safety barrier or warning sign. He'd plunged straight into the culvert and hit his head on the steering wheel in the impact. Given my experience with the hole next to the phone box I could well believe the story. He was now awaiting a negligence compensation payout from Townsville council. Helena was shorter than him, well rounded, with brown eyes and short blonde hair. Jason was a handsome, alert, blond-haired little boy. Given that Jack wasn't the best-looking man in Queensland, and nor was he Jason's biological father, the gossip was that Helena was only with him because of the prospect of the payout.

35

Jack and Helena slept in their car and Helena made up a little bed for Jason in the annex. If he was at all bothered by Tess – an animal that was three or four times his size – it wasn't obvious. The next morning I was making some tea in the kitchenette when Helena appeared at the caravan door and asked me if we had any eggs. We did, and she asked if Jason could have one for breakfast along with some toast fingers. I said sure and that I'd have one too and that I'd cook them if she made the toast. I got a pot out of the cupboard under the sink, filled it with water and took the eggs out of the fridge and put two eggs in the water and put it over a flame on the little stovetop. Jack was still dozing. Helena called to Jason to come into the caravan and sit down. She got a glass down from the other cupboard and filled it with water. I would have given him a glass of juice but we didn't have any: we only had the basics. Jason sat at the bench table and chairs. They were quite small and so a good size for him. Helena went out to the car and came back with a small grey ceramic eggcup in the shape of a koala's face, with little protruding ears on the sides, and sat it down in front of him. He smiled and chuckled. It was so unusual to have someone around who was concerned with somebody else, rather than just obsessed with their own needs and wants. The next thing she did was put some toast on, and then make a mug of tea and take it out to Jack in the car. Small bubbles were rising from the bottom of the pot so I turned the flame down a little and checked my watch.

Helena came back in and pulled the pieces of toast that had popped up out of the toaster, putting two more pieces of bread in and pushing the lever down. She put them on a plate and I got the tub of butter out of the fridge and put it on the table. She took a knife and began to butter the toast, then cut the pieces into thin strips. Jason was busy driving a matchbox car, which he must have slept with, all over the table. It looked to me like James Bond's Aston Martin. That's a nice car I said, what is it? He looked up and answered me, It's James Bond's car. I'm going to be a secret agent when I'm bigger. I laughed and remembered the time my parents had taken me to see *Diamonds Are Forever* at the drive-in and my mother had given me a lecture afterwards about how she hoped I didn't think that going to bed with one woman after another was a good thing to do or any way to live your life. But she didn't say anything about not using an ejector seat to shoot people out of your car.

I checked my watch, three minutes had passed so the eggs would be soft boiled, I hooked one out with a spoon and placed it in the eggcup. Then I realised that there was no eggcup for my egg, as there wasn't one in the caravan cupboard. So I cut the end off the egg carton and put my boiled egg into one of the empty spaces. That's very clever said Helena, while placing the egg and koala cup in front of Jason. I was a bit embarrassed and blushed a little and didn't say anything in return, and I put the kettle on again and got out the teapot to make us a proper pot rather than just mugs. Helena put the toast fingers in the middle of the table and picked up a knife and sat down next to Jason. Now sweetie, she said, I'll just take the top off the egg and then you can make a volcano. She cut the top off the egg and said There you are. Err yuck yelled Jason, it's all white! Ok, ok, she said, I'll get rid of it. I passed her a teaspoon and went back to making the pot of tea while she carefully scooped out the white from the top of the egg, exposing the gleaming yellow yolk.

I put a couple of tea bags in the pot and filled it with the boiling water. Then I put my makeshift eggcup on a plate, grabbed a teaspoon and sat down opposite them. I picked up the knife and took the top off my egg. I like the white, I said, and spooned some out with my teaspoon. Urr, it's horrible, Jason complained. Well, it's gone now, his mother said, so it's time to make a volcano! Yay, he shouted, and picked up a toast finger and plunged it into the egg. Molten yoke spilled out of the shell and ran down over the koala's head. Wow! I said, what a great volcano. I picked up a toast finger and plunged it down into my own egg and said, Some people call these soldiers. Which people? asked Helena. I dunno, I replied, the English, but fingers is a nicer name. She smiled at me and again I blushed a little more. Sorry, I said, I didn't ask you if you wanted one. That's ok, she said, smiling again, I'm a big girl, I can look after myself, I'll just have some toast. Right, I said and got up to pour us some tea. I put the mugs back on the table. Is there any honey? she asked, No, sorry, I said. Because Jason likes honey in his tea, don't you darling. He nodded. We'll get some next time we go to the shop, I said.

At this point Jack came up the step and into the caravan holding his mug and asked, Is there any tea left in that pot? Yes I nodded. He poured himself some and sat down next to me, opposite Helena and Jason. I finished my egg and downed my tea and decided that I would brave the mozzies in the shower block. I went over to my bunk and picked up my towel and toiletries bag and went out into the annex. As I walked away from the van Gordie sidled up to me and said, You know that slut Helena's only after Jack's money. I glared at him. But he hasn't got any money, I said. No, he answered, not yet.

36

The next day we all went in to Townsville to check in at the CES and then went to see the Tannenbaums. The dogs loped up to Jason in the backyard and began to sniff and snuffle over him. Helena put a protective arm around him and they scampered off. Jack, Gordie and the brothers talked over the usual subjects, people they had in common, like Charlie Varafakis, Dave Voss and Dave Smithton; the rest of us sat under the palm trees. Jason had brought his Aston Martin with him and drove it up and down the table. I wondered what had become of Lucky; gone back to Charters Towers I supposed. Helena said to Jack that it was time for Jason's lunch. I suggested the fish n' chip shop down the street. The three of them got up to leave saying that they'd see us back at the van. The rest of us decided to stop at the supermarket and do some food shopping. There were matchbox cars in the toys aisle, and I found a red Porsche I thought would go well with the Aston Martin. You crawler, said Gordie when he saw it in the trolley. I didn't say anything to him about the jar of honey I'd also slipped in there.

The Tannenbaums had told us that Crystal Creek, where we'd had the mango fight on the way to Hidden Valley, flowed down out of the ranges towards Townsville, and that near the bottom was a pool that was great for swimming. The next day we decided to go up there and have a look. We followed a bush track that led off the mountain road and arrived at a beautiful, round, pristine pool with sloping rock sides and a cascading cataract at one end. We parked the cars and got out. The rock wall was lower on this side and it was easy to get into the water. Gordie, Alka, Al and Lachlan pulled off their shirts and dived in. I watched Helena take off her yellow dress and step down into the cool, clear water in her black knickers. Jason stayed on the side with Jack, who apparently couldn't swim very well. Kevin didn't want to go in either. I pulled off my singlet and jumped in. We all swam towards the small waterfall on the other side. I ducked under the cascade and came up for air, letting the falling water massage my neck and back which was a bit sore from so much driving. I swam over to a low section of the rock wall and pulled myself out of the water climbing up to the flat top where I could turn around and sit and look at the pool and the bush. Helena was treading water just near where I had climbed up, her breasts bobbing up and down just below the surface. Help me up, she said, extending an arm out towards me. I kept looking at her but made no move. What is it? she asked, Are you shy? No I'm not, I said uncomfortably, looking away. She paddled over to the rock and I bent down to give her my hand. No, you don't seem like shy boy to me she continued. She took my hand in her wet fingers and I pulled her up onto the rock. She sat down next to me and shook her head, drops of water splashing on me from her hair. It felt nice. Even though I'd only been out of the water a few minutes it was so hot and humid that I was already dry.

I looked across to Jason and Jack on the other side. Had Jack noticed? What was he thinking? We sat on the rock, chatting. I asked her about Jason's father. She had met him at a party and he'd left six weeks after Jason was born. He wasn't interested in me after Jason was born, she said. Silly bloke, I added, But Jack has obviously got more sense. She smiled at me, and I thought I should change the subject, so I asked about when Jason would be going to school. He would be turning five soon, so next year, after they'd found somewhere to settle down up here. Actually, she said, I better go back to him. She stood up and jumped off the rock and into the water and began to swim over to the other side. The boys were bobbing around under the waterfall, so I jumped in and went and joined them.

It was quite a little paradise: clean, clear, mountain water to swim in; gorgeous, big, smooth blocks of granite to relax on and rich eucalypt bush all around; lucky that Townsville was where it was, and that the colonists hadn't decided to move in here instead. We all swam back to the other side. Helena had brought a sandwich and a bottle of water for Jason but the rest of us had been so excited about coming for a swim that we hadn't thought to bring anything for any sort of a picnic. Let's go to the pub, said Jack. An hour later we were playing pool and drinking pots of XXXX.

Lachlan announced that he wanted to go back to Sydney for a few of weeks. For the past few years he had been enamoured of our mutual friend Silvana. The problem was that it was difficult for Lachlan to get time alone with her. Al was keen on her too, but for Silvie, it was obvious that the choice between the handsome, gregarious Lachlan and the eccentric, socially inept and uncomfortable Al was not a difficult one. So Lachlan reasoned that if he went home, leaving us all in Queensland, he would be able to cement their relationship without interference, or so he told a version of this to me. He also wanted to take Tess, technically his brother's dog, home, as she was proving increasingly difficult to manage in the course of our itinerant life. So the next day, I took him in to Townsville and we went to a travel agent and he bought a ticket on the next morning's Ansett flight to Sydney.

We got up, had breakfast and I drove him to the airport. Al, Alka and Gordie came with us. We checked Tess in, had a beer at the airport bar, and then he was gone. Having had a taste the four of us stopped at Rollingstone for another beer on the way back. A few beers later and it was mid afternoon and we left the pub and headed back to the caravan. We'd had enough to drink to make us what old people called 'merry', so I stopped at the bridge. Bullshit, said Al as he peered over the rail at the long drop. He hadn't been with us the first time and he thought the idea of jumping a bit preposterous, but we convinced him it wasn't dangerous. Gordie jumped in to demonstrate, and Al thought about it for a few moments and went over himself. I followed him and we swam to the shore and climbed out and sat down together. It was Alka's first time too, but he climbed onto the railing and executed a perfect dive, plunging headlong into the water with the sort of neat splash an Olympian would have been proud of. As he walked up the bank shivering from the cool water I said, That was pretty brave Alk. He grinned his crazy grin and said, as he sat down, Thanks, yeah, I hit my head on the bottom but it didn't hurt too much. I reasoned that this couldn't make him any sillier than he already was.

We went back to the van and cooked some sausages for tea. It was a very warm night so we moved the table out of the annex and sat outside. Jack went for a shower and came back wearing his towel, which he took off and put over a chair, and sat down facing away from the table. He and Helena had bought some marijuana off the Tannenbaums and she rolled a joint, which she lit up and passed to him. He sat there in his naked, pale, mostly hairless body, looking at the dark van park, his indolent penis flopping between his legs, as he puffed away at the joint, appearing as if he didn't have a care in the world. From inside the van Jason called out Mummy, and Helena took another quick drag before passing it to me, then going in to him. I pulled the smoke into my lungs and looked up at the stars, silent, twinkling and abundant.

37

The park managers were asking that we pay some money, so we thought the best thing to do would be to leave. Al, Gordie and I wanted to drive up to Cairns, to see what things were like up there. Kevin and Alka wanted to come with us. Jack and Helena wanted to go and camp out at Crystal Creek. We agreed to meet them there the following week. The next morning we packed up the cars and drove off, waving to the park manager as we drove out of the gate. We turned right and headed up the Bruce Highway. It was a beautiful tropical morning, grey-green mountains to our left and ahead of us and behind them a dazzling, depthless blue sky.

We drove north, through seemingly endless fields of sugar cane until after about an hour we came to the town of Ingham, a name synonymous with chickens in Sydney but to which there was no connection up here. We didn't stop as we hadn't been going long and drove out of town into more cane fields. Soon the road began to run along the coast, passing through a town with the charming English name of Cardwell-by-the-Sea. The highway was set right by the beach and a long string of neat little fibro cottages sat staring out to sea, waiting for the next cyclone. We were listening to the local pop music radio station and the announcer said that this day was Lou Reed's thirty-sixth birthday. I was quite chuffed to hear this, as it seemed to connect us with the world in some ineffable way. In fact, this information was wrong on both counts: if it *had* been Lou Reed's birthday, which was not actually for another few weeks, he would have been thirty-nine, not thirty-six, but in those days I tended to believe what men on the radio said. Inspired, I leaned across and fished around in the glove box for the tape of *Rock'n Roll Animal*, which I found after a bit of one-handed driving, causing us to swerve across the centre line and Gordie in the passenger seat to shout out Fuck me in alarm. I pushed the tape in and the opening notes of the intro to *Sweet Jane* by guitarists for hire Steve Hunter and Dick Wagner began to blare from the car's speakers. It was such a monumental piece of music that neither Gordie, Kevin nor I said anything for the next ten minutes or so as we cruised through the fields of cane and bananas.

Lou Reed made me think of Pazza, Stephen Parry. Pazza loved Reed's *Coney Island Baby* and we'd once spent an evening on acid at Kevin's listening to it. Pazza particularly loved the opening line of the title song where Reed sang, or recited really, You know man, when I was a young man in high school you believe it or not I wanted to play football for the coach. Coming from Lou Reed this was just about the most memorable thing Pazza had ever heard, beacause Pazza loved playing rugby league. And he also really loved Reed's other great passion: heroin. Indeed, it was together with Pazza that I first tried heroin, the Queen of drugs in those days, in his bedroom in the shed in his parent's backyard. I'd trusted Pazza with the operation rather than any of the other useless junkies we knew because he was comparatively sensible and reliable: despite his persistent habit he managed to hold down his job as a bricklayer as well as turn up for training every week and run onto the field for the game each weekend. In the quiet of the shed he cooked it up in the spoon, loaded the syringes and offered the first one to me. He tightened the belt around my arm and found the vein and pressed the needle in. It was a bit much, and soon I was lying on the floor looking up at him as he demanded to know: Mate, are you alright? Yes, I am, I replied through the haze. That's good, he continued, because if anything had happened to you I might get charged with murder. Fuck me, I thought, he didn't say, I was really worried about you thinking that you might be dead, but instead it was standard junkie self-centredness. So then he had his shot and said it was good and we went over to the house in Sans Souci where Al and Lachlan were living and sat around a fire in the backyard and drank beers, and just like Lou Reed said I didn't care anymore about all the Jim-Jims in the town and all the politicians makin' crazy sounds and everybody puttin' everybody else down.

It was a perfect start on heroin for me, almost losing my life, because it made me realise that despite how good it made you feel it didn't make for a very promising career path. Once at a party on a cold winter night in the backyard of Lachlan's cousin's place in Newtown someone asked Pazza what the difference was like between heroin and marijuana. Mate he said – as we stood around the keg of beer, he in his winter trademark flannelette shirt over a Bonds t-shirt – it's like the difference between eatin' chocolate cake and drivin' a Vdub. He loved driving a Vdub, a Volkswagen beetle, he owned one, but he liked chocolate cake even more. I really liked Volkswagens too, but I think I liked them even more than chocolate cake. Pazza died a decade or so later, aged 36. His mother found his stiff, cold body one morning out in his shed bedroom. Whichever so-called friend he'd been with the night before had rifled through his wallet and then left without calling an ambulance.

The next town was Tully, after which the eponymous 1970s psychedelic rock band had been named. It was known as a place where it rained a lot. Fittingly the blue sky of morning began to fill with big, fat dark grey clouds. Just as we reached Innisfail, about three quarters of an hour later, rain began to land on the windscreen in big splattering drops. I knew that Innisfail, like Ingham, was a place to where lots of Italians had migrated early in the century to work cutting the cane and bananas: Maria back in Moranbah was from Innisfail. It was lunchtime and so we pulled over in the main street and ran to a café on a corner that had tables out front sheltered by big sheets of canvas and umbrellas. As a change from tea I ordered a cappuccino together with what the menu called an Italian sandwich: ham, cheese and tomato on toasted square, flat, white bread. Little did I realise that in a few years I would learn to call this focaccia and that together with coffee it would become my standard lunch option in various coffee bars around Sydney.

After lunch we got back into the cars and continued towards Cairns. We crossed a river and to the left the road began to skirt some mountains while on the right were more cane fields; after not too long stately

Queenslanders, mostly painted white, began to line the road as we passed through the southern suburbs of Cairns. We stopped near the centre of town and reverse parked into angled parking spaces. There was a pub on the corner. We went in and sat at the bar. They served the local brew, NQ Lager, rather than the omnipresent XXXX; also of note were the bar staff: women who all wore see-through negligee-style tops. The woman serving us was deeply tanned, had long brown hair and shapley large-nippled breasts on display under her black chiffon shirt. Although I'd never seen anything like this in Sydney I guessed it was supposed to indicate city-style sophistication in this regional capital. I thought it was crass and ridiculous, but no matter how much I tried to avert my eyes they kept drifting back to her breasts as they jiggled each time she bent over to pick up a fresh glass or pull the handle of the beer tap.

She wasn't in any way hostile to us, but nor did she smile or try to make conversation or appear to be enjoying herself. We asked her where we could get a pizza and she said there was a nice place a short walk down the street. We found it and ate our fill, and then went looking for a school verandah to sleep on.

38

The next morning we were sitting on the promenade that ran along the main beach looking at the sea. I was getting tired of being afraid to go in the water and said so. Alright said Gordie, standing up and pulling off his shirt, let's go then. I stood up and pulled off my t-shirt too and we gingerly waded into the warm, soupy water. With each step we took I was feeling more and more nervous. I just couldn't bring myself to dive under and potentially come face to face with a box jellyfish. When we reached waist depth, Gordie said, I've had enough, and turned and headed back to the shore. I did too. Next to where we were sitting there was a council worker, a red-faced, middle-aged man with a fat belly, picking up fallen palm fronds and throwing them into the back of a ute. He laughed as we emerged from the water, and said, You cunts must be fucken mad goin' in there! Gordie smiled at him and said, Yeah mate, I s'ppose you're right.

I sat down next to Alka and put my arm around him and asked. You ok Alk? I'd been sleeping next to him on the school verandah and had woken up to the sound of him sobbing. I asked what was wrong and he said, I was dreamin' that a beautiful sheila was kissin' me and huggin' me and cuddlin' me. She just wouldn't stop kissin' me and cuddlin' me. Then I woke up and she was gone. Well never mind, I said, at least you've still got your mates. He kept crying, and rolled over to face the other way.

We drove up into the mountains to a town called Kuranda. It was famous for a scenic railway for tourists, which ran along the cliff tops through the rainforest that covered the area. We went to a takeaway and had hamburgers for lunch, and then went to look at the railway station, which was extremely picturesque, decorated with lush green ferns in hanging pots and so on. We thought about going on the train, but in our dirty, smelly clothes and being shaggy and unshaven we didn't feel comfortable amongst all the clean and upstanding mums and dads with their neat little kids, not to mention the obsessively neat and tidy Japanese. This combined with the fact that you had to pay money for a ticket decided us against a train trip. There was a large waterfall nearby so we went to have a look at it. It was the wet season, so the falls were in full flood. The water didn't fall over a sheer drop as in the conventional image of a waterfall, but rather cascaded down over tiers of sloping rocks in a massive display of churning power. The air was damp and filled with a cool light mist: a wonderful antidote to the constant heat.

When it finished its downward plunge the water emptied into the bottom of the gorge, forming a small lake that again became a river flowing towards the coast. It seemed a good idea to go down to the bottom where we could have the swim we had been denied having in the ocean. There was a picnic area at the bottom of the gorge next to the river. We parked the cars and went into the water and paddled and floated around the edge. I looked up at the verdant rainforest covering the sides of the gorge and the blue cloud-tossed sky behind and wondered how life could get any better. Al pulled me out of my reverie by challenging me to a race to the other side. It was about fifty metres across so I said, Sure. We paddled around and lined up and Kevin called out, Go! I dived forward and thrust underwater for the first few moments, then surfaced and swam as hard as I could. I found swimming in clean fresh water difficult, it didn't seem to have the slight thickness of the ocean or chemical-filled pools. As it was I could see when my head came up after each stroke that Al was pulling ahead of me. Soon he reached the other bank and climbed out of the water, raising his arms in the air above his thin, scraggly body like he was Rocky Balboa. I slackened off the pace and leisurely swam up and sat down next to him, sucking the fresh air deep into my lungs.

We dried off and got back into the cars and drove back up over the mountains onto the Atherton Tablelands. We headed to the main town, Atherton, which lent its name to the surrounding area. Like many Australian towns, a war memorial featuring a statue of a First World War digger dominated the main street. These figures usually held themselves in heroic poses, but this one, in what seemed to me a particularly Queenslandish flourish, appeared to be cooeeing to his mates. We stopped and had a look around and went to the supermarket and bought some eggs and a couple of packets of chips. Alka went into the Commonwealth Bank to see if his Sickness Benefit allowance had been paid. He came out with fifty dollars and we sent him straight into the bottle shop with instructions to buy a case of beer and a bottle of rum. We waited outside the elegant, old, two-storey pub. It was a wooden construction, probably from the nineteenth century, painted white with balconies all around. Behind it the sun was nestling into the silver clouds on the horizon, in preparation for drawing the day to a close. The sound of people laughing and enjoying themselves wafted out from the public bar. What would you do, Gordie asked, if they were about to drop the bomb and everything was gonna end in five minutes? I dunno, I said. He continued with an answer to his own question, I'd grab the nearest sheila and say How about it? He smirked. I looked at him in silence, I couldn't think of anything to say.

Alka came out of the bottle-o with a carton of NQ stubbies and some Bundaberg Rum, and said, I was gunna ask for a case of beer, a bottle of rum *and* a bottle of scotch, but I didn't have the guts. We all laughed and Gordie said, You piker.

We consulted our map of North Queensland and saw that there was a small national park at a place called The Crater not too far south of Atherton, which looked like a good place to spend the night. We got there just as it was getting dark, finding a small car park and picnic area. We sat down at a picnic table and drank a few beers, Gordie complaining that NQ Lager wasn't as good as XXXX. None of us was particularly hungry so we made do with the packets of chips and then passed around the bottle of rum. Eventually we got our sleeping bags out of the cars and laid them down on the grass. I slept very well.

39

In the morning we got out the billy and Al's primus stove and boiled up some water for tea. The crater in question was the remains of a volcano, so after we'd drunk our tea we followed a path through rainforest that came to a platform overlooking a big hole in the ground. It was round and about 100 metres deep with sheer granite sides. The bottom was full of water the top of which was covered in some type of aquatic weed a shade of bright, pale green. The effect was an amazing combination of severity and placidity. Gordie picked up a couple of rocks and hurled them over but the pliant green surface swallowed them without comment: he would need more than stones to make his mark on the landscape here.

We went back to our camp for breakfast, filled the billy up with more water and boiled some eggs. After they'd cooled down we peeled and ate them, sitting at the picnic table, then made more tea. It was a grey, humid morning, and Gordie voiced his desire to do what he called 'bakeoffs', which after some explanation turned out to be what circus people called breathing fire. He wanted to go to a hardware shop to buy some sort of petroleum-based propellant, like kerosene, or paraffin if they had it.

Looking at the map there was a town nearby called Ravenshoe. It had been established as a centre for timber cutting and sawmilling and supposedly named after a discarded novel found in the area, surely the only such instance of this in Australian history. We stood in the main street looking up at the town hall, a beautiful big building in a style I would later learn to identify as Modernist and made out of bricks despite the fact that Ravenshoe owed its existence to the popular local activity of tree killing. More in keeping with local history there was also a big old wooden pub, with timber porticos all round to keep the white, European-skinned patrons safe from the serious tropical sun. There was also, much to Gordie's satisfaction, a hardware shop, within which he was able to purchase a one-litre bottle of kerosene. We went to a café for morning tea (they had scones!), and the waitress told us that there was a beautiful waterfall called Millaa Millaa further south which was definitely worth visiting.

If the Barron Falls up at Kuranda were nothing like the conventional idea of a waterfall, then Millaa Millaa Falls were the complete opposite. In fact, they could have served as the ideal waterfall in Plato's realm of perfect forms, so orthodox were they in design: a thick, uniform stream of water fell like Rapunzel's hair straight down a twenty metre drop into a round, placid pond. The double name indicted an Aboriginal term for an abundance of something, but of what I had no idea. I was contemplating a swim in the pool while Gordie opened his bottle of kerosene and placed it on a wooden picnic table next to a disposable lighter. He picked up the bottle and took a swig, his cheeks puffing out as his mouth filled with the noxious liquid. Then he picked up the lighter, flicked it on and spurted out a jet of kerosene just above the flicker. Accompanied by a whooshing sound it burst into a blaze of orange and yellow flame. He spat on the ground and said Fucken hell. Then he did it all again. It was an utterly pointless though spectacular and no doubt bodily satisfying activity. I looked at him standing there in his blue shorts and his Sex Pistols t-shirt which he never seemed to change or wash and it appeared as if his way of being was totally geared to the satisfaction of one kind of physical want or need after another. I wondered if we were all like this to a less extreme extent. Here we were in this sublimely beautiful place and all Gordie wanted to do, rather than enjoy its beauty, was to turn himself into some sort of absurd stunt act. I took off my clothes and went and dived into the water and swam out to the waterfall and dived under it, coming up with the fall of water hammering on my head.

Gordie continued with his so-called bakeoffs, but after he'd done a half dozen or so, he stopped; no doubt it was quite tiring. But whatever demon it was, he had gotten it out of his system, and he put the lighter back in his pocket and the top back on the bottle of kerosene.

There was a village also named Millaa Millaa nearby, where we found a takeaway shop, had something to eat and then went back to the falls to sleep the night. The next morning we had another swim, made some tea in the barbeque area and then drove down the road to Innisfail, where we stopped again for coffee and Italian sandwiches. Then we headed south to Crystal Creek to hook up with Jack and Helena and Jason. We found them camped by the creek some distance down from the pool where we'd swum previously. It was a good campsite so we decided to stay there. Jack and Helena and Jason were sleeping in the back of their car. They had a small two-man tent set up, but Jason didn't want to sleep in it because he was afraid that animals would creep into it in the night, so Kevin and I elected to sleep in it instead. I asked him what sort of animals he was afraid of and he said Tigers. I laughed and told him there were no tigers in this jungle, and that being so close to the water the only thing I was afraid of was mosquitos, but he didn't look reassured.

We were all tired, and we went to bed as soon as it got dark. The tent had no flyscreen so I placed a mosquito coil at the entrance, which meant falling asleep to the smell of its noxious fumes but that was better than being bitten. In the morning we cooked up some bacon and eggs on Al's primus and then went for a swim in the creek. The water was quite fast-flowing which was good since we hadn't had much opportunity to wash lately. I climbed out and looked down the shallow valley through which the creek flowed. The water shining silver in the morning light, the light grey rocks at the side of the stream and the deep green of the tropical bush all gave off a sense of the beauty and wonder of being alive. Jason wandered up and sat down next to me and I told him I'd kept an eye out all night for tigers, but that I hadn't seen any. He said, Good. This was because there might not be any tigers around here. I wondered what it was like for him, getting dragged around from place to place with no order in his little life, but things could be a lot worse I reasoned: he could be stuck in an ugly suburban house with nasty, violent parents; maybe being on the road with happy-go-lucky drug users wasn't too bad.

A golden honeyeater was warbling on a branch above us and we both looked up at it. He asked me if I knew about how dinosaurs had turned into birds. I said yes, millions of years ago some small dinosaurs grew wings and found that they could fly around. He said, wow, he wished he could see those dinosaurs with wings, so I pointed at the honeyeater and said, look, there's one there. He laughed and stood up and jumped up and down on the spot a couple of times, which was what he did when he was excited. I wanted another cup of tea, so I got up as well and we walked back to the camp together.

We all went to Townsville in the afternoon and called in at the Tannenbaum's. They invited us to a barbeque on the coming Saturday night. This seemed a very civilised prospect and I almost forgot for a moment that I was living in a tent in the bush, and went back to the camp excited at the prospect of a social event.

40

We didn't do much over the next few days, just pulled bongs, smoked joints, swam in the creek, walked in the bush and sat around our little camp talking. There wasn't anything we wanted and there wasn't anything we needed. On Saturday afternoon Jack, Helena and Jason left early and went in to Townsville to a supermarket to get some steak and sausages for the barbie. The rest of us piled into my car a bit later and stopped off at the pub to pick up some beer. While there we drank a few rounds and had a couple of games of pool, then about five o'clock we headed to the Tannenbaums. Jack, Helena and Jason were already there, sitting in the backyard when we arrived. Cracking open our beers, we sat down with them, the dogs running around snarling and panting as usual. Jason was playing with his cars and talking to himself about them; he was remarkably tolerant of the dogs. I remembered that when I was his age I was scared of dogs.

Peter fired up the barbeque and Hans – who seemed the most domesticated of the three brothers, (perhaps, ironically, this was the reason he had problems with their mother) – began organising the food. There was a long wooden table with benches that we all sat down at. Hans put a plate of small pieces of steak and a plate of sausages on the table, then went into the kitchen and came out with a loaf of bread, a tub of margarine and some tomato sauce. Karl followed him out with plates and knives and forks. We all served ourselves. Helena put three sausages on Jason's plate and cut them up and squirted some sauce over them. Yum he said loudly.

I forked a piece of steak and a couple of sausages onto my plate and waited for Gordie to finish with the sauce. Steadying a sausage with my knife, I stabbed its lightly charred skin with my fork and a jet of hot liquid spurted out and splashed onto my white Bonds t-shirt. Fucking hell I said, as those who'd noticed chuckled. Never mind, you can wash it in the creek tomorrow said Helena. Jason jabbed at a piece of his sausage trying to get the same effect. Oh no he whined when nothing happened. I moved onto the steak – fresh north Queensland beef – which was delicious after not having had much to eat over the previous few days. I felt guilty about eating animals that had been killed and cut up by other people, and thought yet again that I should stick to fish, though I didn't say anything about it as the Tannenbaum's home didn't seem the ideal place to agitate for a vegie life-style. So I buttered a piece of bread, put a sausage on it, squirted on some sauce and rolled it up and took a bite. That was the main problem with eating meat: it tasted so fucking good!

Helena went into the kitchen and brought out the tub of chocolate ice cream she'd bought at the supermarket. Karl fetched some bowls and spoons. Yumm said Jason, stretching out the word. Eat all your sausages, his mother told him, before you can have any ice cream. Obviously he'd get some I reasoned, as it had no doubt been purchased specifically for him. Mummm he moaned, but then dutifully gobbled down the contents of his plate. Helena spooned some ice cream into a bowl and put it before him. Soon his face was covered in brown smears, looking like a Hollywood Indian's war paint.

The rest of us pushed our plates away and sucked on our beers. Thanks boys, said Gordie, raising his XXXX in salute, though it was Helena who deserved thanks as much as the brothers. Hans reached across the table and clinked his bottle against Gordie's. Karl had saved a piece of steak and he lifted it from his plate and handed it to Satan who was nosing around his legs. We continued to sit around drinking while it got dark. As usual in the tropics within a half hour or so the sky was a deep blue black. Hans brought out a mixing bowl and a bong and Jack made up a mix that passed around the table. It was good stuff and after a single cone and a bit of coughing I found that I was quite out of it.

Peter stood up and said Right, time for some movies. He collected some of the plates and cutlery and carried them into the kitchen. Hans and

Helena cleaned up the rest. We made our way to the long verandah room that ran along the back of the house. There was a super 8 film projector set up facing towards a screen at one end of the room. We slumped down on the old lounges that made up the room's furniture.

Apparently the brothers documented their tree killing work on film. This should be interesting I thought; I'd always liked films shot on super 8. I liked the grain of the image, and the dark and shadowy light and palette. It made for very melancholic pictures, something about the silent flickering image spoke to me of death and of the passing of time. The first images were of a beautiful green forest. Then we saw Hans and Peter smiling and smashing their axes into firm, healthy brown tree trunks. Next one of them took over the camera to record Karl squirting poison into the gaping wounds on the trees. I'd read about so-called Snuff films in which people – usually porn film actresses – were murdered in front of the camera, but nobody was sure if they really existed or were just an urban myth. But this, which we were watching here in suburban Townsville, was real enough: tree Snuff, the killing of an ancient, pristine landscape to make more grazing space to make more steak and sausages like we had just eaten.

Karl guffawed and said Show 'em the keg! Ah, not the keg moaned Peter. Yeah, go on, urged Karl. While Peter looked through the pile of spooled films in the cabinet under the projector Hans explained how at the time of Karl's birthday a few months earlier they had bought a keg of XXXX and taken it out on a job with them. Ok, the keg, said Peter holding up a reel and loading it onto the projector.

The first images were of the keg sitting in the back of their Nissan Patrol. Peter was using the stainless steel gun and length of hose that you got with a keg to fill plastic glasses with the frothy amber fluid. Then there were some scenes of the boys sitting around their portable camp table toasting and guzzling the beer. Hans broke in with some narration. Apparently they ended up drinking the entire 9 gallon keg over one afternoon and night and hadn't really had much to eat while doing so. So the next day with nothing inside their bodies except beer they had developed serious cases of diarrhea.

The next shots in the film showed Hans and Peter sitting up in trees and spurting wild jets of liquid faeces out of their arses towards the ground. At first it was hard to believe we were watching this, but the display went on until the end of the reel of film, Karl had just kept on filming it. I'd never seen anything like it, as the sickening brown spurts filled the screen. Under other circumstances it could have been seen as some sort of bizarre form of performance art, but there was nothing circumspect or motivated about it, it was just spontaneous vulgarity. Gordie and Jack guffawed and groaned, Al, Alka and Kevin stayed silent. So, that was the keg, said Karl mischievously. Helena stood up and grabbed Jason's hand and dragged him out into the kitchen. I followed them. Jason looked confused. What do you think of that? she snarled at me and then continued, I think it's just disgusting. I agreed that I thought it was pretty awful too. What's wrong with you men, she asked? I don't know I replied. Sorry. She turned to the sink and poured Jason a glass of water from the tap. Would you like one? she asked me as she handed Jason his glass. Yes please, I answered. Then they went back out to the verandah and I stood in the kitchen alone, drinking my glass of water.

Peter showed no more films. Hans made a big pot of tea and put out a plate of chocolate biscuits, of which Jason was only allowed one. I guzzled my tea down by way of straightening up after the beer and bongs so that I could drive us back to our camp. The stars were bright over the creek when we arrived. Kevin and I crawled into our little tent and then into our sleeping bags after I lit a mosquito coil. Soon Kevin was snoring quietly and I lay on my back listening to him and the sound of the creek bubbling by outside. I couldn't get to sleep. I just couldn't get the awful images of the shit squirting down from the trees out of my mind. As Helena said it was just disgusting. The Tannenbaums seemed to have no respect for the world around them whatsoever. But how was their attitude any different, on a vulgar and personal level, to the actions of Wolfgang and his machines back at Moranbah: ripping the earth to pieces to gouge out coal so that it could choke the atmosphere with sulphur and carbon dioxide?

Eventually I managed to get to sleep. I woke up the next morning and

Kevin was sitting up in his sleeping bag looking at me. Mate, he said, when he saw I was awake, I want to go home, I'm sick of it up here.

41

Al and I thought that we would like to make another trip up to Cairns and further north. I persuaded Kevin that he should come with us and then go home afterwards. He thought that was a good idea.

Gordie on the other hand didn't want to come. He had organised to move into the spare room at the Tannenbaum house; so a couple of days later I drove him into Townsville. We stopped out the front of the house just as Karl came down the street on his motorbike. He pulled up, climbed off, took off his helmet and said G'day. We stood at the tailgate of the Ford as Gordie collected his small bag of possessions. Karl inspected the contents of the back of the car and pulled out the hammer I kept in there. You can use this to hammer the car if it won't go, he said. Gordie laughed and lifted out my axe and held it up What do you think of this? It looks old, Karl replied. I explained to him that it had belonged to my grandfather who had grown up in the bush near Canberra, but he didn't seem very interested, and Gordie put it back in the car.

See ya, he said and pulled out his bag and headed into the house with Karl. I got in the Ford and drove away and never saw him again. When I got back to the camp I noticed that he had left his black felt jacket in the car. It had Tooths written on the back in white letters and he had acquired it while working at the Tooths Brewery at Central in Sydney. It was a very punk-looking item. I thought about dropping it in to him at the Tannenbaums but I had always coveted it, and anyway, I reasoned, it never got cold enough up here for him to need it, so I decided to hang onto it. I ended up losing it myself a few years later, leaving it on the platform at Munich railway station. Like many German railway stations in the 1980s, Munich *Hauptbahnhof* was infested with junkies, so it would have found a good home.

We drove north again the next day, leaving Jack, Helena and Jason at the creek, telling them we'd be back in a week. Again we stopped at Innisfail for an Italian sandwich and cappuccino and then continued on to Cairns for afternoon tea at a café. The skies stayed clear; it was getting towards the end of the rainy season.

Port Douglas was a small seaside town, nestling in the coastal rainforest, and nothing like the concreted, multi-storied, global tourist hotspot it would become in the 1990s. We pulled up next to the line of early century, verandahed timber buildings that made up the main street. It was starting to get dark and we were standing by the cars considering where we would spend the night when a golden brown-haired young woman with a light brown dog – either Labrador or golden retriever – panting at her side walked by. She was very tanned and wore a long cheesecloth shirt, and had obviously been giving the dog a run on the beach, which was at the end of the road. She stopped, said hello and asked, Have you guys just come into town? Yes, I said, amused by the idea that this place was so small that everyone here knew who everyone else was. She asked where we were staying and we said we didn't know and she said she had room at her place and did we want to stay with her. She said her name was Julia and directed us up the street and around a corner and down a narrow driveway. She lived in two rooms that made up a breezeblock structure under a house on steel stilts.

We took our sleeping bags into her spare room. She asked if we were hungry, and proceeded to heat up a pot of dahl she had on the cooktop. Al volunteered to go and get some beer and asked did she want some? No thanks, she said, but could he get a cask of white wine? Kevin and I sat down at her kitchen table while she fed Skyler, the dog. I asked her a few questions by way of making conversation. She was a chef at the restaurant in the hotel. She was from Perth. Her best friend had died in a car accident a year ago and she had come over to Queensland to get as far away as possible from all the things that reminded her of him. I said that was sad and she looked at me in silence for a few moments and said well, anyway, it was like paradise here, and if things had turned out differently she wouldn't be here, would she? I said that seemed like a good attitude, and she gave a brief laugh that might have been sardonic and then got up to stir the dahl. Kevin stayed quiet; he was no great conversationalist at the best of times and, pale-skinned and fat, girls usually scared him unless he was drunk or out of it or both.

Kevin's weight really worried him, and a year or so ago he had managed to lose a lot of it. He had gone on a diet and run obsessively, usually wearing, under a football jersey, a garbage bag with holes for his head and arms, which made him sweat like he was in a sauna. He continued to play rugby league, which we had all played at school, but he switched from playing in the forwards to fullback – a lean, fit man's position. I went to watch a couple of his games, watching him zealously patrolling the empty space between the rest of his team and the goal line, gathering the ball when the opposition kicked it through and sometimes aggressively running it back into the middle of the field, but usually kicking it back with a big up and under like he had seen famous fullbacks do at Kogarah Oval or the SCG or on television. He made for a reasonable fullback, but the thing was, he had been a great front rower – a big man's position – a talent he had squandered for the sake of trying to be someone he wasn't. But it didn't last – Kevin's flirtation with the number 1 jersey – soon he was overeating again and piling on the kilos and no amount of slogging it out around the streets in a garbage bag could keep him at the back of the field. His parents divorced around this time: his father, Mr Peacock, a sulky Scottish engineer, had lost his job at a factory, but couldn't bring himself to tell Mrs. Peacock and continued to pretend to go to work, spending his days sitting in parks reading newspapers. Eventually she figured out what was going on, and the marriage went the way of his job. They sold the family home, a fibro cottage near the airport, and Kevin and his sister moved into a house with their mother a few suburbs away. Mr Peacock got a better job than the one he'd lost and made a new life for himself: he'd never seemed to like being a family man very much anyway. Developers bought the house and demolished it and those around it and built a hotel to service the airport. I missed his little house, the lounge room was a place where we had taken a lot of drugs and listened to a lot of heavy metal records. Kevin went and took a room at the hotel after it opened, and spent some time, as he put it, in the space where his bedroom had been.

These fleeting thoughts from the history of Kevin were passing through my mind while he sat at Julia's table and she stood at the stove and stirred the dahl, when suddenly Alka came running in with a look of panic on his face and saying that I needed to come outside quickly because Al had crashed his car. I jumped up and followed him, Kevin trailing after us, thinking fucking hell, why did things like this always have to happen, why couldn't I just be left to talk to a beautiful woman while she cooked me a meal?

Consistent with Alka being no sort of reliable witness, Al hadn't actually *crashed* the car. There had been a big downpour of rain an hour or so earlier that had turned the driveway to mud and the Holden had partly slid sideways and the two wheels on the driver's side had become bogged in the side garden of the next door house. Al had the panel van in reverse but no matter how much he revved the engine the rear wheels just spun in the mud and it stayed put. Kevin, Alka and I got on the front and pushed while Al cautiously applied the accelerator. Slowly the vehicle began to shift backwards and soon we had it back on an even keel; calamity averted. Thanks boys, said Al as he jumped out and went around to the tailgate and retrieved the carton of NQ lager he'd brought back from the bottle shop. Hallelujah, with Gordie no longer present we were free to drink something other than XXXX. I pulled out the cask of moselle he had gotten for Julia and we went back inside.

I put the wine cask down on the table and Julia said oh, great thanks. Having carried it in and deposited it made me feel as if I'd played some role in providing it, which of course I hadn't. She asked me would I like some and I said sure, why not and, as she opened a cupboard and took down some plastic tumblers, she asked if anyone else wanted some wine, but the boys all said no thanks, leaving me looking – hopefully – as if I was the only one on her level. I was pleased that Lachlan was back down south, as he would have been doing everything in his power to hit on her, as would have Gordie; but, with the three stooges I was left here with being so inept in dealing with women, I knew I could relax and enjoy her company.

She held up the cardboard box, and said with a laugh, you know we Aussies invented this, and poured us both some pale yellow wine. The moselle, as it was called, was warm and sickly sweet, but it went down well enough (I was years away from the *Puligny Montrachet*-loving snob I would eventually grow into). Julia got out a soup server and four bowls and filled them with the yellow green lentil mash and put them on the table along with a plate of plain flat bread. We each took a bowl and sat down and she passed us each a spoon before sitting down herself. Have some bread, she said. This is naan bread isn't it, I asked, where did you get it? I made it, she said in a matter of fact way, her big green, grey or blue eyes staring at me without blinking. Great, I said, taking a piece of it and tearing it in half.

We ate our dahl and talked about life in Port Douglas and north Queensland. I got to the bottom of my bowl and used torn up pieces of naan to mop it up. Actually, I wasn't that familiar with Indian food – I'd only ever had it a couple of times before – but I acted as if I was. Julie poured me more of the Moselle, but after a few more cups the sugariness got too much for me and I took a beer from the fridge. After weeks of living in a tent, broken only by the ugliness of the Tannenbaums' barbeque it was blissful to be sitting around a table eating and drinking. Julia seemed to be enjoying it too, though it was hard to imagine there wasn't better company than us on offer in the town. Why had she taken us in? I finished my beer and got up and got another one.

We finished our dahl and sat drinking and talking for a while longer. After some more moselle Julia collected the empty bowls from the table. I stood and went to the sink and began to fill it with warm water. I squirted some dishwashing liquid into the water and watched it bubble up. Julia deposited the bowls and utensils into the foaming water. She asked me if I wanted rubber gloves and I said no thanks. Oh, a tough guy, she said. I put the first clean bowl in the drying rack next to the sink and Al asked for a tea towel to dry up. Julia said not to worry because in this heat things just dried by themselves.

It had been a long day so after we had finished the washing up I emptied my beer and said I was going to bed. Julia stood up and said she was going to have a shower. Within minutes we were in our sleeping bags on the floor of the other room. The wall between the two rooms was made from cinder blocks laid on their sides, and you could see through the openings to the main room, so when Julia came out of the shower wearing a towel you could see her moving about tidying things up. Alka and Kevin were positioned next to the wall and I could see them keenly peering through the hollows waiting for her to take off her towel before getting into bed, but suddenly she reached over to the light switch and flicked it off and that was the end of the show for the evening.

42

I slept soundly until morning. It was amazing how nice a floor could be if it was in an agreeable place. Julia got up and I could hear the sound of her putting the kettle on, so I climbed out of my sleeping bag and went in and asked if it was ok if I had a shower. Of course, she said. I went and grabbed my towel and my small toiletries bag and went into her bathroom and shut the door. I pulled off my shorts, slid back the nylon shower curtain and reached in and turned the taps on. It was such a steamy morning I considered having a cold shower, but given that I'd been living in the bush for a couple of weeks I decided I should take advantage of this opportunity for a proper wash, so I made the water lukewarm and stepped in and stood under the jet. I had no shampoo so I lathered my hair up with soap, which took a bit of effort as it was tangled and matted. I did the same with my beard and then soaped under my arms, between my legs and the rest of my body. I stood for about five minutes letting the tepid water cascade over me. Then I stepped out and dried myself, wishing I had something to put on other than a pair of shorts that needed a wash. Dirty shorts aside, I walked out feeling like a new man.

A half an hour or so later we were all sitting around Julia's table sipping our morning cup of tea. She turned on the radio and the signature tune for ABC radio news blared out: bah-bah-bap-bap-bah-bah-bah-diddle-diddle-dee, a sophisticated bugle call for the bourgeoisie. THIS IS ABC NEWS, said a mellifluous voice laced with authority, not unlike Robert's down in Kempsey: The Alice Springs Coroner has found Azaria Chamberlain was taken by a dingo and that no member of her family was responsible for her death. We all looked at each other and smiled. Fuck, said Kevin, so the dingo did it. We all had a bit of a chuckle. I felt something of a sense of closure to what had been such a long-running saga, with no idea that it would now grind on for decades – through four more inquiries and even dragging the Hollywood actress Meryl Streep into the story – before Lindy Chamberlain was finally acquitted of having killed her daughter.

Al had bought a loaf of bread and some butter when he'd gotten the beer, so we made toast. Generous as Julia seemed to be we needed to make a contribution. She asked me if I would mind driving her over to the other side of the town to pick up something, a girl she knew who lived there was leaving and had told Julia that she could have her collection of cacti. I said, of course, you would have had to be a real dickhead to have said no after all the kindness she had shown us. Ok, she said, I'll just get ready. She rummaged through a basket of clothes and then went into the bathroom and I could hear her turning on the shower. We were still drinking tea when she came out twenty minutes later in a pair of denim shorts and a grey singlet top which showed off her muscular arms and shoulders, her hair a slick, wet mane that cascaded down her back. We were probably quite smelly, because she asked the boys if they wanted to do some washing in her machine and hang it on the line out the back while we were gone. That would great thanks, said Al. I got up and went into our room and put on my spare pair of shorts and a singlet, leaving my dirty clothes, which hadn't been properly washed for weeks, on top of my sleeping bag. I asked Al if he would put them in for me, and Julia said to him, Come on, I'll show you how to use the machine, and he dutifully followed her out the back. Next he had to move his car, which was behind mine, so that Julia and I could get out.

I backed out of the driveway and Julia gave me directions. Tessa, as she was called, lived in a house near the wharf on the west side of the town. I was driving like Elvis, looking at Julia as she talked rather than at the road. Yeah, she went on, I met Tessa at Yoga. She's a bit of a space cadet, but she's nice enough. Yoga, I was thinking as I looked her up and down, well anyway, that explained her arms. We stopped outside a white-painted wooden house and got out and went up to the front door, Julia carrying a cardboard box in which to put the plants. She knocked on the door and a young woman answered it. Johnny Rotten said never trust a hippie, of which Gordie was constantly reminding me. The hippie era was well and truly over but nobody seemed to have told Tessa, someone whom neither Johnny nor Gordie would ever have trusted: thick and wavy dirty blonde hair, a thin cheesecloth shirt over very large, round breasts, a purple, tie-dyed sarong and bare feet (most locals appeared to go around barefoot). There were rings in her ears, a ring in her nose and she had a tattoo of a mermaid on her right bicep (this was long before tattoos became fashion statements, but rather signified their bearers as being outside of society as Patti Smith put it). There was also on overwhealming smell of patchouli oil (of which I was very familiar because Silvana wore it a lot). Yis, she said hillo, come un.

Julia introduced me and Tessa gestured for us to come in, leading us into the lounge room and pointing to a couple of chairs on either side of a wicker coffee table. She took Julia and her cardboard box out to the backyard, which, she said, was where the cacti luved. She came back after a minute or two and sat down opposite me. There was a small lacquered box on the table between us and she leaned forward and opened it, taking out an already rolled joint. She picked up some matches from the table and lit up, taking a long drag and then passing it across to me. As I inhaled I could tell that it was quite strong, obviously good quality stuff. I passed it back across the table. So, you're moving, I said. Yis she answered, I'm going up to Cape Trub. To where? I asked, never having heard of anywhere by the name of Cape Trub. Cape Trub, she said again in an annoyed tone, as if I was deaf or a halfwit. But then the penny dropped: she had such a thick New Zealand accent that I hadn't understood that she meant Cape Trib, Cape Tribulation, so named by Captain Cook because it was the place where 'all his troubles began'. The dope was obviously affecting me, because I was musing that it would be good to have a precise geographic point to which you could assign all your problems. Yis, she continued, I've got a friend up there. He says I can live there for free if I hilp hum out with thungs. What sort of things? I asked. She held up the joint between drags and said He grows dope. Right, I replied, that must be a bit of a risky business. She smiled, It's ok, he's got a gun.

At this point Julia came in from the backyard with her box of succulents, which was good because the conversation had taken a course I didn't really want to pursue. Tessa offered Julia a drag of the joint but she declined, so we said goodbye and took the box out to the car. Julia said there was a nice café at the wharf and suggested we go there for a coffee, as it was just around the corner, so we put the box in the car and drove down to the waterfront.

We parked and walked over to the wharf, a white-painted timber structure from the beginning of the century. There was a heritage panel which explained that the wharf had been built to ship gold from diggings inland at what was now the town of Chilagoe and that after the gold dried up sugar had been exported from Port Douglas. The historic storage building had been destroyed by a cyclone in 1911 and then rebuilt a few years later. So here it was again, the same old story, Port Douglas only existed because men had wanted to rip stuff out of the earth to make money from it. We sat down at a table and looked out at the shimmering blue water of the inlet that formed the town's harbour. The waitress approached and said hello to Julia. They knew each other of course, and we ordered two coffees. Further along the waterfront from where we sat was the spot from where well-heeled tourists traveled out to the exotic resort of Lizard Island, which Julia told me was said to be Prince Charles' favourite place in the world. I didn't know what to think about this – Charles sponging in the sun on one of our islands – as I considered myself a republican. Lucky Prince Charles, I said, and thought about the fact that I still hadn't seen the Great Barrier Reef myself. I told Julia and she said shame on you and that that Green Island off Cairns was worth visiting. It was surrounded by coral and you could go there as a day trip. Good I said, I'll talk to Al about it. She laughed, and said Really, I don't know how you put up with those boys, they're brats. Yeah, I said, nodding my head and feeling embarrassingly disloyal. I asked her how old she was and she said, twenty-six. I asked her why she hadn't smoked any of Tessa's marijuana, and she said that she didn't like smoking dope because it made her paranoid. I told her that Black Sabbath's *Paranoid* was Kevin's favourite song. She laughed again.

We finished our coffees and Julia suggested we go for a walk. Along the foreshore we came to a church, which, like the wharf, was made of timber and painted white. A sign said St. Mary's by the Sea. It reminded me of the timber gothic-style churches in the New England states of the USA which I'd seen pictures of. Julia pushed open the door and we went inside. It was quiet and cool, a nice change from the hot morning outside. We were alone and we sat down in a pew at the back. Julia knelt down and closed her eyes and clasped her hands together. I wished that I could talk to God too, but I didn't know how to. After a few minutes Julia sat back on the bench again. Come on, she said, we better go and make sure your mates are under control and haven't flooded my house. We got up and left. I asked her what it was that she had prayed for but she wouldn't tell me.

Back at her house everything was ok, they hadn't wrecked the washing machine or caused it to flood the laundry, and our clothes were rapidly drying on the line on which Al had hung them. We took it easy that afternoon. Julia rounded up her dog and said she was going down to the beach, which was what, she said, she always did on her days off work. Work not being something we needed to concern ourselves with, we hung around reading and drinking cups of tea. Later Kevin and I went for a walk to the beach. It all looked very tropical, clouds were billowing out on the horizon.

There was still plenty of dahl left, so Julia asked us if it was ok if we ate it again, two nights in a row. Sure we said, it was certainly better than having to make something ourselves. Anyway, I really liked it though I usually felt tired after eating it, I think my body found lentils hard to metabolise. So we repeated the night before, sitting around the table drinking and talking. Julia eventually got up and went for her evening shower. We were all a bit tired, and Al, Kevin and Alka called it a night and went into the spare room to get into bed. I stayed at the table finishing my beer. Julia came out wrapped in her towel and sat down on the edge of her bed and we began to talk, mostly about her ideas for opening her own café. Suddenly she stood up and looking me straight in the eye she pulled off the towel and stood naked in front of me with a wry smile on her face, as if to say, well you wanted to see this, so here you are. I continued to sit at the table holding her gaze for a few moments. She had a beautiful body and I couldn't stop looking at her, and I knew that the boys would have been peering through the bricks at her, and she probably knew it too. She turned and pulled back the sheet and climbed into bed looking very pleased with herself. I stayed at the table and we kept chatting as if nothing had happened until she said, I'd like to read my book now, and I got up and went to bed.

43

We had resolved to leave the next day, and we packed up the cars after breakfast. Julia pulled me aside and said, You can come back anytime, but not your friends. Sure I said, see you soon.

Rather than head straight back down the coast we went north following the Captain Cook Highway as it ran up and over the ranges to the west of the town. We stopped at the top, where the view looked out down to the town of Mossman. We got out of the cars and sat taking in the view. The valley below was filled with the almost iridescent green of sugar cane fields, glowing in the mid-morning sun. Out to the east was the warm, languid blue of the Coral Sea. It was a vision of paradise such as I'd never seen before. But as taken with the beauty of it as I was, I couldn't stop thinking about Julia's beautiful naked body. She was the first woman (as opposed to girl), that I had ever seen naked, and the fullness and strength of her bare form had stunned me. The line of her hips, her flat but slightly curved belly, the line of her ribs, the firmness of her large breasts and the sense of self-possesion she seemed to radiate had pretty much taken my breath away as I sat at the table feeling like a boy very much out of his depth.

I stopped day-dreaming and let the view of the land envelop me. It might have looked like Eden down there but I knew that there was nothing natural about this bucolic haven, it was a landscape that had been created so that men could make money from it. Hard-working labourers, probably from islands in the Pacific, had sweated to cultivate and harvest the cane that had then been exported as sugar from Port Douglas. But despite this awkward history the physical beauty still brought a smile to your face. We went back to the cars. At this point the highway turned to the north and another road branched off taking us down through the Atherton Tablelands and back to Cairns. This enchanting vista marked the most northerly point to which we would venture.

When we got to Cairns we went to the wharf from where the ferry to Green Island sailed. There were three trips a day so we booked tickets for the 9am service the next morning. Then we went and had a beer and a pizza – welcome after a couple of nights of dahl – and went and found a place to sleep. We got to the wharf in the morning in time to hire snorkels and facemasks. To save money (the deposit was more than the rental fee) we only got two sets, which we could share. The trip out took about an hour. After weeks of driving around it was great to be out on the water, with someone else in charge. We were inside the ocean barrier of the reef so the pale blue water was calm and placid, with the occasional flurry of warm spray thrown up from the bows.

The island soon came into view ahead: a small clutch of green rainforest and low-slung, cream-coloured buildings surrounded by white sand, sitting alone in the middle of the sea. The ferry pulled up at a long timber-decked wharf that jutted out from the beach. There was a holiday atmosphere as the ferry disembarked; like us, most people on board had come out for the day rather than to stay in the high-priced resort, and there was a feeling of excitement in the air as the passengers walked towards the island and their first experience of the Great Barrier Reef.

We walked around (you could walk right round the island in about twenty minutes), until we found a café and had our breakfast/morning tea. Then we went down to the beach with our snorkelling gear. Al and I adjusted the mask straps to fit them to our heads. Every place seemed as good as any other so we walked straight out into the water adjacent to the piece of beach we were sitting on. We spat on the glass and then rubbed the saliva around and rinsed the masks out with seawater to stop them fogging up, then pulled them on.

Diving under really was like entering another world. It was hard to know where to look, the reef was all around us, and was as psychedelic as a night on acid. Bright orange towers rose up from the sea floor, where cool green nests of living rock shapes proliferated, interspersed with glowing yellow and red outcrops. Slender cobalt blue fish wove in and out of the open spaces. I thought of Ringo Starr and his octopus's garden. It was an underwater Eden, even more spectacular than anything up above, and what's more, there were no box jellyfish to worry about as apparently they didn't like reef environments, but preferred the coast. I looked ahead to Al paddling around nearby: he pointed down at a giant clam and then gave his head as much of a little shake of disbelief as he could (being underwater with a snorkel), as if to say, Bullshit, look at that!

We swam back to the beach to give the other two a turn. We sat down on the sand in the bright morning sun, and Al fished around in his day bag and lit up a smoke. There was a woman in a bright red bikini sitting on a towel nearby. She looked over at us and then leant back on her arms offering herself up to the sun. She looked over at us again, looking us up and down and then lay back down and rolled over onto her stomach. Eyeing her, Al exhaled a cloud of smoke and said, It wouldn't be a bad life, working in a bank all year and then coming here for a week or so. You reckon? I said, smiling, finding it impossible to imagine him doing something similar.

Kevin and Alka came out of the water raving about the things they'd seen and sat down. We stayed sitting in the sun talking for a while about how incredible the reef was, then repaired to one of the island's bars for lunch.

We ordered the cheap meals from the menu and ended up getting quite pissed, then went back and did some more snorkelling: what all the rule books say you should never do, swim after eating and consuming alcohol. We took the last ferry back to Cairns. I was standing at the rail looking out at the sea while next to me a red-faced bloke in his forties or fifties, with a big belly inside a Hawaiian shirt, smoked a cigarette. When he got to the end he flicked the butt over into the pristine water. Hey, I said, don't do that to this beautiful place, why couldn't you put it out on the deck? He turned his head towards me and snarled. You ignorant fat cunt I said, it jumped out of my mouth before I'd even had time to think about it. He looked at me with a mixture of shock and contempt, as if he wasn't sure whether to stab me or ignore me. Then he harrumphed again and walked away into the cabin. The sun had dropped down behind the mountains behind Cairns, the western sky a blazing mix of orange and red. Off towards the horizon the gentle sea was darkening into a rich inky blue. It was all so beautiful and fragile; I crossed my fingers in the hope that we would be able to take care of it.

44

Kevin had had enough and when we woke up the next morning said I want to go home today. So I took him to Cairns airport and waited while he booked a seat on the next flight to Sydney. Then I drove back down to Townsville. Kevin might have been a big fat bloke, but emotionally he was very sensitive and complex, and he'd been out of sorts ever since the Tannenbaum's barbeque and film night, the vileness of which had obviously been too much for him, even though he'd never said anything about it. Kevin loved the Pink Floyd song 'Fearless' from their album *Meddle*. Dave Gilmour (Kevin's favourite member of Pink Floyd) sings 'You say the hill's too steep to climb' and then answers, 'but you name the place and I'll pick the time', indicating that he'd 'just wait around 'til the right day'. 'I'll climb that hill in my own way', he concludes. Kevin loved these lyrics and would often recite them. I imagined he felt that at many points in his life he'd been told that the hill was too steep for him, and he'd gathered his own fearlessness from the knowledge that because he wasn't like everybody else he too could attempt the hill in his own way, at a time when he felt like it. We had a coffee at the airport café and I left him waiting to board and walked back out to the car. 'Fearless' ends with a recording of a Liverpool football crowd singing 'you'll never walk alone': I always felt as if I was letting him down, and this was no exception, but he was hard going being mentally ill most of the time, and I generally had enough trouble just looking after myself. So I left him alone waiting to go back to what ever was in store for him at home.

It was a pleasant experience driving back to Townsville by myself. It gave me plenty of time to think, not that I had much to think about. I wondered if I should turn around and drive back up to Port Douglas and go back to

159

Julia's as she had suggested. But the more I envisaged her beautiful naked body standing before me, the more scared I became at the thought of having to confront it again. Really, it seemed so much easier and less threatening to just go back to my mates. Al and Alka were already at our campsite at Crystal Creek when I arrived. Jason ran up to me as soon as he saw me and asked if I had another toy car for him. I told him sorry, I didn't, and I wished that I'd been thoughtful enough to have had one for him. Jack and Helena said that nothing interesting had happened while we were gone. Nothing had been seen of Gordie who was obviously as happy as a proverbial pig at the Tannenbaums' where the XXXX would no doubt have been flowing.

We went to the pub for tea and phoned up Lachlan who, having consolidated his relationship with Silvana, was ready to come back, so we organised to pick him up from the airport in a few days. Back at camp we didn't do much apart from swim in the creek. I took Jason for walks in the bush, where we checked out the birds, trees, ants' nests and other interesting stuff. Once we saw an echidna; it rolled itself into a ball for protection and Jason got so excited he jumped up and down a few times. Al went to the airport and picked up Lachlan and brought him back. Having missed our trips to Cairns he urged us to make another one. As nice as it was at the creek we were all getting a bit sick of living in the bush. Helena thought we should find a house to rent, which would make looking after a little boy much easier. So we agreed that the best thing to do would be to go back up to Cairns and look for a place around there.

It had been a good time to leave the camp because by the time we got to Cairns the sky was a murky grey. Our three vehicles were angle parked in a street while we sat on a low fence outside a medical centre and debated what to do. The radio news had said a cyclone was about to hit the coast. Wind and showery rain swirled around us and the street's trees bent over so far they looked as if they would break in half. As we watched, a violent gust of wind grabbed hold of the back of Al's panel van like a giant fist and gave it a shake. I looked at everyone and said I think we need to get out of here before something bad happens. We all agreed the best thing to do would be to head west up to the tablelands and get away from the coast before the cyclone hit.

By the afternoon we were in the hills on the road to Atherton. The sky was still grey but the wind hadn't reached this far inland. We pulled over at a rest stop and agreed the best option, as we were passing by farm after farm, would be to stop at the next house and ask if they knew of any houses for rent. Amazingly we were met at the door of the first place we tried by a red-faced man in a grey hat, who told us that in fact the next house up the road from him was available. Where are you blokes from, he asked us? Sydney or Melbourne or one o' them places down south? Sydney, we said in unison. He laughed.

The property next door was a former dairy farm, the cattle long gone. Apparently the owners were two German food scientists who worked in Melbourne for Kraft, the American transnational cheese company, and who only came up during the Melbourne winter, so we could have the place for a few months: just off the main road was a medium-sized tin-roofed house, white paint peeling from its solid timber boards. We wasted no time moving in. There were six bedrooms and a pile of mattresses stacked in one of them. We each picked a room and dragged the mattresses into the rooms, dumping them on the naked floorboards. In the kitchen there was a big, old, cream-coloured kerosene-burning stove. I'd never seen anything like it before, but in a few years time I would learn that they were very popular amongst the rural middle classes in Britain. We had no kerosene, which was ok, because we had no food to speak of, except for some biscuits and cheese for Jason.

We went to Atherton the next morning to transfer our Unemployment Benefit registrations to our new address, and to buy some food and kerosene. We went to the Department of Social Security and the CES and went through the bureaucratic rigmarole necessary to being officially unemployed. Yes, of course we were looking for work in the area. We went to the hardware shop and got some kerosene, for a much more productive purpose than for Gordie's so called bakeoffs. Then we went to the supermarket and got some potatoes and beans. We bought a carton of beer. There was a fish shop on the main street so we pooled the last of our money and bought eight pieces of barramundi.

That night Jack and Helena boiled the potatoes and beans and fried up the fish on the kerosene stove. They dished them up on a plate in the middle of the kitchen table, which we were all sitting around. Helena served Jason the smallest piece of fish and then we all took one. None of us had had a decent meal for a while and we were all desperately hungry. Our eyes followed the fillets of barramundi as they moved around the table, each of us wishing that we could have more than one piece. Jack had cooked it well: the skin was really crispy. I finished my piece, took a swig on my beer, and looked at the empty plate in the middle of the table, as did everyone else. At least there were plenty of potatoes. Jason didn't want all of his barramundi so Helena took what he left, which was only fair enough, she was his mother after all. Eventually the meal kicked in and our hunger subsided as we drank the beer. We went to bed early and I fell into a deep peaceful sleep.

I woke as bright sunlight spilled in through the window and across the brown floorboards. It was great to be in a bedroom in a real house. I got up and went out to the kitchen to make some tea. Jason was already running around amusing himself. Going through the utensils drawer for a tea strainer I found a black-framed magnifying glass. Hey Jason, I said, look at this! He ran over and I handed it to him. He got very excited, jumped up and down and immediately ran out the back door and down the sandstone steps. I finished making my tea and took it outside to join him. I sat down on the steps as he jumped around on the grass looking at things with the magnifying glass and talking to himself about them.

I took a sip of tea and looked up at the pristine blue morning sky and thought about how wonderful it would be to be able to get so excited about something as simple as a magnifying glass. I had been there myself once, but as Peter, Paul and Mary sang in *Puff the Magic Dragon*, 'dragons live forever but not so little boys'. We all had to grow up sometime, although maybe Wolfgang with his mining machines was not so far away from Jason, just that the things *he* was passionate about were bigger and wreaked more havoc. I looked down at a trail of small brown ants on the step below me and called Jason over. Look at these ants I said, they are making a trail down the steps from the kitchen and down to wherever their nest is. Watch this, I said and asked him for the magnifying glass. I focused the sunlight through the glass until it became a bright spot of light, then I trained it like a laser beam onto an ant, which sizzled into a burnt little speck as a brief burst of smoke rose up. Wow, said Jason. Do you want a go, I asked. Yes please he answered, and I passed him the glass. He quickly got the hang of focusing the sunlight into a point and began frying the ants, something I'd spent many happy hours doing when I was little. No doubt about it, boys really loved destroying things. I tipped out the dregs of my tea and stood up and went back up to the kitchen.

45

This being a former dairy farm, there were dried up cowpats all over the place. And where there was cow shit, we reasoned, there would also be magic mushrooms. After breakfast Al and I went out the back and walked around on the grass having a look. Jason had grown bored with incinerating ants and gone back to using the magnifying glass the way it was designed to be used, which was good because I felt a bit guilty about having taught him such a cruel trick and I was also a bit worried about him inadvertently starting a fire. It didn't take us long to find a few pale mushrooms with the requisite light brownish golden domes. Wow, usually the finding of magic mushrooms involved quite an expedition, risking the wrath of irate farmers as you trespassed on their property and so on, but here they were literally in our very own backyard! We gathered them up and brushed the dirt off the stems and dropped them into the plastic container Al had brought out from the kitchen. We left Jason to his observations and went back inside. I got out a cooking pot, filled it with water and placed it on a hob on the stove. Al dropped the mushrooms into the water and stirred them around with a wooden spoon as we waited for the water to boil up our brew. Pretty soon we had a pot full of brown liquid and I scooped out the drooping fungi with a strainer. We filled up a teapot and got down some mugs and called everyone out to the kitchen. Helena took a look out the back to see what Jason was up to, then we all sat down at the table while Al poured us each a mug of mushroom tea. Lachlan raised his mug and said Cheers and we all took a swig.

I'd only ever had gold-topped mushrooms once before, a couple of years earlier when Lachlan, Al and I were staying at Noosa Heads. We had headed out one sunny morning to farmland on the road from Noosa to Eumundi, 'up Eumundi Road' as the Queenslanders referred to it: a low-key zone of mixed-use farms that would no doubt nowadays be sub-suburban housing. We'd pulled over and jumped over a post and rail fence and began scouring the grass. Al was concentrating on searching the ground meticulously, and so failed to notice the brown bull charging towards us. I had already turned and begun running back to the fence by the time I called to him. He looked up and yelled Fuck – which showed how rattled he was, because he rarely swore – and took off at a sprint for the fence, which he got to before me. We both threw ourselves over it to the safety of the road and left the disgruntled animal panting and snorting on the other side just like in a Bugs Bunny cartoon.

Such is the commitment of true drug addicts though, that as soon as we'd gotten our breath back we sped across the road to the field opposite and climbed the fence into it. Bugger that, said Al, there were some good mushies in that paddock. Almost instantly a circling grey and white bird plunged down out of the blue sky at us and let out a shriek, then flew upwards, did a circuit of the field and then repeated its dive-bomber act. It was a plover that must have had a nest nearby and was trying to scare us off. It continued to circle and swoop us – the wildlife of the area seemed determined to frustrate our quest for hallucinogens – but since the plover never actually made contact with either of us with its beak, but only screeched at us – which was still pretty disconcerting – we took our time looking through the paddock, and came away with a cap full of gold-tops.

We drove back to H's house at Noosa and gave the mushrooms a quick rinse under the tap and ate them as quick as we could rather than going to the effort of boiling them up.

For want of anything better to do we drove down the beach to wait for the mushrooms to come on. I was starting to feel a bit tingly so I walked off on my own. I walked along a bit until I came to a big swarm, or whatever the collective noun is, of soldier crabs. They had bright blue bodies and pink appendages and I remembered having seen them on the beach down at Currumbin when I'd stayed on the Gold Coast with my parents when I was a kid. I remembered that I loved pursuing them along the beach, because they would run this way and that, and if you persisted in towering over them they would give up running and burrow into the sand, leaving a neat little pile of damp churned-up sand on the surface above the hole they'd made. So I started following them and if one separated from the cluster they would behave just as I remembered and dig down into the sand, though they mostly stayed together as a group and tried to avoid me. But what really amazed me was that they seemed to move collectively: they would turn left or right as a group, as if they had some sort of collective mind. By this point I was tingling all over and felt ridiculously excited, the mushrooms were obviously working, and the behavior of the crabs seemed to be affording me some sort of profound insight into insect life, indeed into life in general, whereby creatures in a group relied on a form of group consciousness. Of course this was something I could have studied at University if I hadn't been so drug-addled and lazy. Eventually I got tired of the crabs and moved on. Just a little back from the sloping front of the beach was a pond of water. Sitting by it was a young man with a homemade fishing rod, of the sort used by Hucklebury Finn-like characters. He wore rock star sunglasses and had a big mop of curly blonde hair like Robert Plant or Ian Hunter and he was wearing a white singlet and a pair of black and white striped trousers held up by braces, a bit like a circus clown. There was a large tattoo of an astrological sign on his right bicep. He seemed happy with his fishing rod in the pond when suddenly a middle-aged woman standing ten or twenty metres away called to him, Come on Johnny let's go home. Ok Mum he answered in a high-pitched voice, and jumped up, running over to her. The afternoon was overcast, and all of this was illuminated by a vivid glowing light under the purplish grey sky.

I was starting to feel a little confused and I turned away from Johnny and his mother as an elderly man approached me. He had a bent back and a stooped gait and a brown leathery face and a white sun hat on his head and was wearing a thick blue jumper despite the fact that it was warm and humid. Pale pink lipstick was smeared unevenly all around his mouth. You know all about them, don't you he said in a shaky voice, pointing at Johnny and his mother. He shook his head and moved away towards the pond. I wasn't sure if any of these people were actually real and I decided to go back to the crabs, but I couldn't find them, maybe they hadn't been real either. I began to feel quite scared and headed back to the car park. Al and Lachlan were sitting on a bench looking worried. What have you blokes been doing, I ventured? Don't ask, answered Lachlan, while Al looked at me without saying anything. Let's go back home, I said and we walked over to the car. I don't think I can drive, I said. I can, said Al, so I handed him the keys and we got in. The whole idea of this big lump of painted metal moving anywhere seemed ridiculous, but it did. Back at the house Al made a pot of tea and Lachlan put on a Bob Dylan record. It was *Street Legal* – his most recent record after *Desire*, which I absolutely loved and had listened to all through my last two years of high school – and I hadn't heard it before. It was one of his records where the whine of his voice tended to obliterate his words, which, combined with an excessive use of brass added up to a sound I didn't much like. As I sat on the lounge drinking my tea and listening, the blaring saxophone and trumpet became wild, horned animals leaping out of the record player at me. I started to feel very nauseous and scared and put down my tea. The animal sounds were scaring me so much I started to cry: I felt as if I'd lost the ability to tell the real from the imaginary and I began to panic. I lay back on the lounge and waited for the noise to stop. Eventually I stopped panicking and fell asleep for a while. When I woke up I felt a bit better, but I was sure that the people down at the beach hadn't really been there.

This experience really challenged my grip on reality and so I avoided taking mushrooms again for the next few years. But now I thought, what the hell, why not give them another go, even though I could already feel a tingling sensation in my guts as I raised the mug to my mouth. We all downed our mugs and then hung about waiting for the mushrooms to work, but half an hour later I still had the tingling feeling though nothing else had happened: the world still seemed relatively normal. Someone suggested that we should go for a swim at Millaa Millaa Falls; Alka was walking about the house with a mysterious smile on his face and holding a folded towel on top of his head, which was as close as we got to a swim because we couldn't actually get it together to go anywhere. Apart from a bit of giggling, as a drug experience it was a non-event. Maybe the mushrooms weren't very potent which, really, was a relief to me since I didn't want to repeat my previous encounter and lose my grip altogether.

46

All of us except Helena received letters from the Commonwealth Employment Service informing us that a mining company was looking to recruit staff, and requesting that we attend the Atherton CES office to be interviewed. We had to go: if you failed to attend they cut off your Unemployment Benefits.

At the CES we were interviewed by two affable middle-aged men in short-sleeve business shirts, shorts and long white socks, the uniform of the male administrative class in Queensland. I was surprised how pleasant and polite they were, given that we were a bunch of scruffy, long-haired dole bludgers. Still they were corporate recruiters, and I guess avoiding alienating prospective employees was part of their job description. They worked for a mining company and were putting together a team to do some exploration and prospecting for minerals west of Chilagoe, more or less in the north Queensland outback. They were looking for a couple of unskilled workers, the idea was that you would go out bush with a small group of geologists and miners while they prospected for copper, lead or even gold, and take care of their day to day needs. It sounded like a lot of fun, and despite my reservations about capitalists exploiting and ripping up the land I tried my hardest to sell myself to them. I had the lines of The Dingoes' song 'Way out west where the rain don't fall, got a job with a company drillin' for oil, travellin' and a livin' off the land', running through my head all through the interview. We waited around while they made their deliberations, announcing to us afterwards, 'We're quite interested in Mr. Reeves, but we've got some more clients to see, so we'll let you know'. You beaut, said Alka, chuffed that for once he'd made the grade. Fuck me, said Lachlan to me as we left the CES, there's only one of us who's completely fuckin' mad, and he's the one they pick. Yeah, well, I replied, I suppose that tells you a fair bit about them and their job, doesn't it?

We did a bit of food shopping and then headed back to the house. Lachlan drove back with me, and about half way home we came to a sign pointing off the highway to the 'Curtain Fig Tree'. We'd passed it before but this time Lachlan said, Let's go and have a look at it, so I turned off the main road and followed a gravel tributary that led to a small car park. A wooden viewing platform looked out onto a spectacular space in the bush occupied by an enormous old tree with what looked like a veil of tangled brown hair reaching from the top down to the ground. An explanation panel told us that this curtain fig tree was a 'strangler fig', a species which germinated at the top of an older tree and grew out aerial roots which grew down to the ground over hundreds of years, forming a 'curtain', over the host tree, which eventually died under the rapacious presence of the strangler.

I was thinking this was an apt metaphor for the human race in respect of our relationship to other life forms on the planet, but such negativity tended to detract from the majesty of the curtain fig tree and the bush glade it dominated. We stood looking at the intricate tangle of life for a while; you know, Lachlan said wearily, it was when John Lennon got shot that I really realised for the first time that things just happen and you can't do anything about them, that change happens and that's just the way it is. One minute he was singin' his songs and talkin' to Yoko, the next minute he's full of bullets and dyin' on the ground. I nodded. John Lennon had been shot just before Christmas the previous year in New York by a nut obsessed with *The Catcher in the Rye*. Lachlan, who had always been in thrall to male counter culture heroes, had worshipped Lennon, and loved *Catcher in the Rye* for that matter. Yeah, I said, I know what you mean, there was no bringing him back to life, even though he had said he was bigger than Jesus. Lachlan offered the sort of forced, close-mouthed grimace he used when he was uncomfortable with something: no doubt he thought I was being disrespectful, though to which ideal I was unsure. He nodded at the curtain fig tree, Lucky they never found any minerals around here, he said.

I was thinking that we should come back here if we had more mushrooms and they worked, and see what the place looked like. Actually the wraith-like tree reminded me of Lachlan's other great love, *The Lord of the Rings*, which we'd read when we were in Year 11, but he didn't mention it, so we just stood looking for a bit longer. It would have been nice to smoke a joint but of course, we had no dope.

When we got back to the house Al was making spaghetti.

47

We spent our days mostly hanging about the house or walking in the fields. The weather was perfect: warm, dry days, the bright blue sky full of puffy little white clouds. We still had our football and kicked and passed it around out the front of the house, teaching Jason how to handle it, a task which Lachlan took on with enthusiasm. He had always been a superb player, and could probably have been a professional, if he could have been bothered to go to training and to take instruction from coaches and other authority figures.

There were two bicycles in one of the front rooms of the house. Good quality road bikes: the owners being German this made sense, given that the Tablelands, with its rolling hills and good roads was excellent cycling country, not unlike Germany as I would discover in a couple of decades' time. One evening just before sunset Al and I got on the bikes and rode them to the top of the long hill to the west of the house. There were no helmets, in those days you weren't required to wear them, and even if you had been I doubt that any self-respecting German cyclist would have been prepared to. The sun was setting when we reached the top of the rise, an orange disc falling below the mountains further west. As always when confronted with this scene it was impossible to understand that it was actually the planet on which you were standing that was turning away and not the small ball of the sun moving around it. I stared at it until the final glimmer dropped away, always my favourite part of a sunset. The horizon lit up with a yellow and orange glow and a few bright stars came out against the indigo sky. I didn't recognise the night sky this far north. Crickets were chirping in the warm dusk and there was also the sound of frogs trilling and croaking around a nearby pond. An owl hooted a night greeting from a stand of trees by the road.

Without discussing it we pointed the bikes downhill and climbed on, swishing off into the gloaming. We freewheeled under the immensity of the sky into the gathering dark, picking up speed as we went, neither of us touching the brakes. Insects splattered into our faces as we whizzed through the warm air, just as against a car's windscreen. There was no traffic either ahead of us or behind us, and if there had been, we were relying on the drivers having their headlights on, because there was no way they would have seen us, nor we them. Nor, if a kangaroo or possum had wandered onto the road in front of us, would we have had any chance of seeing them and avoiding a spectacular collision, just as a rock on the roadway – at the speed we were travelling – would have meant the end of us. So, mindful but careless of the danger we raced on into the evening, our speed letting us feel as if we were an actual part of the landscape, not just observers outside of it, the exhilaration of the pure moment of being alive exceeding any fear of life as a whole coming to an end in a shattering accident.

We finally hit the brakes as we rounded the bend into the straight that ran along the front of the house, and still there was no traffic. We pulled up outside the front gate and dismounted, our heads spinning, and took the bikes up the front step, parking them in the hallway. We went into the kitchen and got a beer each out of the fridge. Where have you blokes been? asked Alka, and we both smiled at him.

We continued to go to the top of the hill at the end of the day for the rest of the week, until a rainy afternoon stopped us.

48

I talked to my mother from a phone box in Atherton and she told me that she and my father were going to New Zealand for a few weeks and that they wanted me to come home and stay in the house while they were gone.

So, on Friday afternoon I loaded my few possessions into the back of the Ford, shook everyone's hand, gave Helena a hug, tousled Jason's hair and drove away from the house. When I got to the Bruce Highway I again had to consider should I turn left and go up to see Julia, or right and go home. I turned right and stopped at Innisfail to fill up with petrol and then kept going on down past Hinchinbrook Island, which looked serene in the golden early evening sun. By the time it got dark I was approaching Ayr and Home Hill where we'd spent the night with the mosquitos some months earlier. I pulled over when I came to a caravan park because there was something I needed to do. I got out and dug my toiletries bag out of the back of the car and walked across the road to the park. Typically, there was no fence and the brick toilet block was on the periphery of the park. I went inside into the sickening glow of the whitish green of the neon strip light and went up to the row of wash basins and mirrors along the wall. I was the only person in there, which was good. I put down my bag, looked at my face in the mirror and pulled out my scissors. I began to chop away at chunks of the unruly ginger beard I'd been growing over the past few months. Soon I had the hair clipped enough that I could start trying to shave off what was left. I pulled out the shaving brush my father had given me for my birthday a few years earlier and lathered up some foam from the shaving soap I'd been carrying around for months but had never used. My razor was sharp, as it hadn't been used either. I frothed the soap and began pulling at the stubs of wiry hair with the razor. There are few things as frustrating as shaving off a well-established beard, it really is a job best left to barbers. Soon I was bleeding like Norman Gunston. I stopped shaving and went over to a toilet cubicle and pulled a handful of toilet paper off the roll.

I managed to stop the bleeding with the toilet paper and after about half an hour of pushing and of dragging the razor around I could run my hand over smooth, tingling skin. I looked into the mirror at the face of a young man I hadn't seen for some time. I packed up my utensils and walked out into the warm tropical night. I crossed the road to the car, soon I would be feeding Snowy the dog and taking Millie to the shops again. I got in behind the steering wheel, started up the engine, and headed south.

Postscript

A few weeks after getting back to Sydney I found a letter bearing a childlike handwritten address and a North Queensland postmark in the letterbox:

Hello mate

How's things, alright I hope. I'm sending you this letter from Bedarra Island where Lachlan and me and Alka are now. It's a small island off the coast near Innisfail and we've scored a job here painting some luxury cottages for a new resort they're building. Everything is real good, and Alka is enjoying the work and doing a good job.

We were on a pretty tight budget before we got here. We scored $300 off social security but only after our supplies were completely exhausted. If it weren't for Jimmy who lives just up the road, he brought over smokes, a loaf of bread, 5 kg of mince and fresh meat from his Dad's farm, we would have starved. Not to mention the cases of grog we scored on credit down at Millaa pub or the paying of the rent that we had to put off. We were one month overdue plus a $30 debt on a bag of grass we scored off Don, who also lives up the road. Really good grass.

We found this job on the island in the CES in Atherton. The island is owned by the airline TAA and they've had eight new weatherboard cottages built and we're painting them inside and out. It's going really good. Because it's an island we have to live here, in the old resort, which is not too bad. There's not a lot to do here except fish and snorkel but we managed to score a big bag of heads off a plumber who works here and so every night we can relax and have a couple of beers and pull a few cones.

All the best
Your mate Al.

Thanks

Thanks to David Musgrave for supporting my work. Many thanks to Des Matejka for his generous gift of an image from his photo archive for the cover. Enormous thanks to Peter Kirkpatrick for his constant encouragement, his brilliant literary sensibility and relentless humour. And thanks to Mark Cross, who encouraged me to write about this time and these events and for our lifelong friendship. Thanks to Warwick and Alain for being great blokes. Many, many thanks to Sara Knox, for her endless enthusiasm, friendship and respect. And thanks to Jane Goodall for her support of Sara and myself. And likewise, thanks to Chris Abrahams for support and encouragement both on and off the page. Thanks also to Matthew Connell for his knowledge of Townsville as well as many other things. Many thanks to Fiona McIvor for her Faith and help in a difficult time. Thanks also to Lucy Macfarlane for advice on New Zealand dialect. And lastly, thanks to Fiona and to Arthur for making the world seem more marvellous than it probably is.

www.ingramcontent.com/pod-product-compliance
Lightning Source LLC
Chambersburg PA
CBHW021232090426
42740CB00006B/500

9 7 8 1 9 2 2 5 7 1 7 1 7